Yesterday's St. Petersburg

Yesterday's
ST. PETERS BURG

By Hampton Dunn

E. A. Seemann Publishing, Inc.
Miami, Florida

To
DR. JAMES W. PARRISH
Pastor Emeritus
The First Baptist Church of Winter Park, Florida
whose high ideals and strong spiritual leadership and counseling gave the
author inspiration and guidance in his boyhood, as well as in the years since.

Contents

Foreword

Florida people care about their past, as the warm reception of my book *Yesterday's Tampa* proves. People are curious about why we are what we are today, and who did what and when in getting us to this point in time.

St. Petersburg, chosen as an All-American City in 1973, is the twin city to Tampa, sharing much of the same colorful background and history, the same struggles, the same triumphs. And yet, though only 18 miles apart—thanks to bridges built by our foresighted forebears—the two communities are quite different. St. Petersburg is more tourist-oriented than Tampa as it has been most of its modern life, although in recent years it has added some light plants, or smokeless industry.

This pictorial view of the city could not be done without the valuable assistance of my friends: Henry Cox of Tampa Photo Supply Co., who wisely acquired the tens of thousands of negatives of the Burgert Bros. photographic firm, and most graciously provided the bulk of the photos for the *Yesterday's Tampa,* has now turned up many beautiful pictures for *Yesterday's St. Petersburg.* Invaluable also was the kind help given me by Walter Piney Fuller who recently published a fine history of St. Petersburg. He spent hours with me identifying pictures and made available to me many photographs from his own collection. I am grateful for the cooperation of Miss Cindy Stokes of the John B. Green Memorial Collection of The First Federal Savings & Loan Association of St. Petersburg who gave me numerous excellent historical shots.

My warmest thanks also go to the following persons and institutions who helped to complete the visual report on this community: Mrs. Martha Golub, writer-editor of the City News Bureau of St. Petersburg, Mrs. Anna Stockwell, Clerk of the City Council, for her aid in getting the use of the collection of

Mr. Ian Boyer; Photographer Bob Riley, for some beautiful reproductions of old scenes; my old friend Sandy Gandy, formerly of *The Tampa Daily Times,* (now merged with the *Tampa Tribune*), for some rare and significant photos from the past, including some from the Gandy family album; Ralph Reed, reporter and editor on the *St. Petersburg Times* and the *Evening Independent* until retirement, and now curator of the Pinellas County Historical Commission in the County Court House in Clearwater, for some beautiful pictures from the commission's official collection (including a large number from the album of James Hamilton, and from the collection of the late Assistant Postmaster Marcus Edwards); Walt Robshaw, formerly of the *Tampa Times,* and now in the Public Relations section of National Airlines, for helping to document the background story on the founding of National Airlines in St. Petersburg during the depression; Sam Harrington, for some intriguing photos of Webb's City and "Doc" Webb's pulchritudinous Poster Girls; Miss Elizabeth Russell of Fort Ogden, Florida, for a picture of her brother Robert F. Russell with the famed St. Petersburg aviator Tony Jannus; and others.

HAMPTON DUNN

St. Petersburg, Florida
August, 1973

Barnacles, Beaches, Beauties, Baseball, and Benches

As Florida cities go, St. Petersburg is comparatively "new" and a late bloomer. It didn't get a railroad until 1888. And two years after that, the Federal census showed its population to reach the grand total of 273 souls.

Yet St. Petersburg, which has been tourist-oriented for several decades now, was "discovered" by the state's first "tourist" back in 1513. That was the year gallant Ponce de León, the intrepid Spanish conquistador, was probing the coastline of the "island" of Florida. It is reported he anchored his little caraval, the San Cristobal, around Mullet Key to clean the barnacles from his ship's bottom.

Juan Ponce de León on that journey was only exploring this part of the new world. Here at St. Petersburg he got the same rough treatment from the Indians he had received all along the east coast of Florida and up the west coast. On Tampa Bay he was attacked by the fiery Timucuans and used his ship's cannon to defend his party. During this encounter, one of his men lost his life, and thus became the first white soldier to be killed in North America. Enough was enough of this hot reception, and the Spanish nobleman and his crew raced back to the Gulf of Mexico and headed home for a cooling off period.

Eight years later, in 1521, Ponce de León came back to these waters, hoping this time to find a safe spot to settle down. But the Indians were still around, still hostile. One of their well-aimed arrows pierced the body of de León and he was rushed, mortally wounded, to Havana, Cuba, where he died. He is buried in Puerto Rico.

St. Petersburg has not overlooked Ponce de León in its recognition of pioneers. There is a stone statue of him in Waterfront Park where it presides

TIMUCUAN WARRIOR, a drawing based on a sixteenth-century water color after a lost original by Jacques Le Moyne, and supplemented by archaeological evidence. (Fuller)

over one of the many Fountains of Youth which the fiftyish de León found it necessary to discover to quench his reputedly unquenchable thirst.

Before the Spanish appeared on the scene, the slender peninsula which was to become Pinellas County many centuries later, was the peaceful home of the Indians who enjoyed Florida living in a primitive paradise. They were the Mound Builders, and throughout the region are reminders of their stay. Although many of the mounds have been destroyed through the years to provide road building materials, there are still many that can be viewed.

Old residents say there were originally six or seven mounds in the vicinity of Sixth Avenue and Sixth Street, South, in what is known as Shell Park, in St. Petersburg. Still other mounds are to be found at Pinellas Point, Maximo Point, the Jungle, Pine Key, and Weeden's Island.

These Indians were rather smart and obviously most artistic, as was borne out in the findings of a party from the University of Pennsylvania, led by Dr. Frank Hamilton Cushing, in an exploration of mounds in the area back at the turn of this century.

Reporting on the excavations, Dr. Cushing commented: "I do not wonder that the explorers so often marvelled at the beauty of the things the natives possessed. The plummets, pendants and other ornamental and ceremonial objects of stone which we found were among the best products of the aboriginal lapidary's art I have yet seen.

"They were made of a great variety of material, from soft soap stone and spar to hard diorite and rock crystal, from hematite, polished like burnished steel, to clean cut plates of mica and elaborately wrought symbolic objects of copper."

Continuing, Dr. Cushing then remarked on the commerce represented in these finds. "The range of commerce that these things indicated was enormous. There was a fine grained stone derived from the far West Indies, a shell from the Gulf of Campeche, the mica and rock crystal were of the Georgia and Carolina kinds, and the copper had been brought both from Lake Superior and from Cuba, while the dematite and galean nodules were of the kind so often found in Mississippi and Iowa."

Living was comparatively easy for the Indians because of the abundance of seafood in the plentiful waters in and around the peninsula, as well as wild

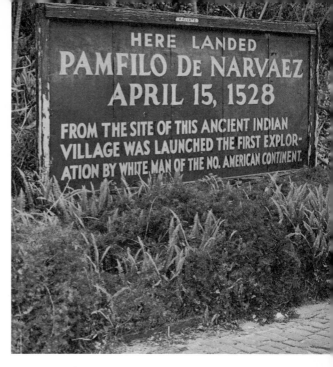

LANDING SITE of Pánfilo de Narváez at historic Abercrombie Park on Boca Ceiga Bay. The feisty, one-eyed Spanish *conquistador* debarked here on Good Friday, 1528. (CNB)

animals in the woodlands. Fruits and vegetables also were easily grown in the rich soil.

Seven years after the debacle of Ponce de León, another important white visitor arrived on the West Coast of Florida. Heading an expedition was the Spanish explorer Pánfilo de Narváez. Then 48 years old, Narváez had already lived an exciting life of adventure in the New World. It was he who helped Diego Valasquez in the reduction of Cuba. And it was he who was sent to Mexico as head of a force sent to the Aztec coast to compel Hernán Cortés to renounce his command. That assignment was tougher than he had expected. In the scuffle with Cortés, Narváez lost an eye and wound up in prison. He was behind bars for two years, but never lost his desire to strike out on his own in the new lands, to plunder and wallow in wealth.

Back home, Narváez got from Charles V of Spain the go-ahead to probe Florida and surrounding territory. The boisterous, one-eyed, red-headed Narváez hurriedly rounded up an expedition to Tampa Bay, It was going to be a huge raiding party. There were 600 soldiers, and the wives of 10 of them were on the trip. Also in this party were the first blacks to enter Florida.

Misfortune enroute was an omen of bad times ahead. From his party, 140 men had deserted at Santa Domingo, another 60 were lost in a hurricane.

Where did Narváez land? It is generally agreed, the party came ashore on Good Friday of 1528. A spindly signboard today tells the world that the conquistador landed in the area known as the "Jungle" on Park Street North, where a large Indian mound exists. The sign says: "From the site of this ancient Indian village was launched the first exploration by white men of the North American continent."

Narváez apparently overshot the mouth of Tampa Bay. There is some speculation he landed at Clearwater harbor. But scholars now seem to settle for the "Jungle" landing site. Walter Fuller believes that this is where Narváez landed; he even erected the sign.

Conduct by this ruthless, persevering, ambitious Spaniard helped to give the white man a bad name with the red-skinned natives. Narváez' public relations were atrocious. It is reported the first thing he did after making contact with the Indians was to engage in a violent argument with the Chief. It is said he sliced a bit of the chief's nose with his sword and, when the Indian leader's mother interceded in behalf of her son, Narváez turned loose his dog on her. Small wonder, then, that the word spread fast from tribe to tribe throughout the state about the invaders, and Narváez soon was persona non grata in the peninsula.

There was other poor judgment on Narváez' part about this time. He sent his ships away, some to Cuba to replenish supplies, and they all were to meet in the northern part of Florida. Mapping was poor and the rendezvous point was not clear-cut. The land forces never got back with the ships. They roamed through rugged terrain to about present-day St. Marks, where they put together some crude sailing vessels and took off in the Gulf of Mexico. Only four persons survived a storm which wrecked the ships, including Cabeza de Vaca, the expedition's high sheriff who kept a narrative of the party's experience. It was he who first put into writing that Tampa Bay is "the best port in the world."

From the Narváez expedition emerged a love story similar to—but long preceding—the romance of Pocahontos and John Smith. An 18-year-old crewman named Juan Ortiz had been on a mission returning to Cuba from the St. Petersburg area. On the trip back, he and three other messengers were lured by Indians purporting to be friendly. Once in camp, the chief executed three of the white men and had doomed young Juan. But the chief's wife and his beautiful young daughter pleaded for his life. It was spared. Juan grew into manhood in the Indian camp. A few years later, in 1539, when Hernando de Soto arrived on the West Coast, Ortiz made contact, escaped, and served as guide for the DeSoto expedition.

Once again, there is a long standing argument as the where DeSoto put in "somewhere on the West Coast of Florida." In 1939 on the 400th anniversary of his arrival, Congress decided to determine once and for all where the landing site was. A team was sent down from Smithsonian Institution and it decided DeSoto landed at Shaw's Point, on Tampa Bay, just west of downtown Bradenton.

Others continue to argue. A writer in Fort Myers, Rolfe Schell, claims DeSoto landed at Charlotte Harbor, moved over to Lake Okeechobee and up the center of the state. But Walter Fuller argues vehemently that DeSoto landed first at Mullet Key, where popular Fort de Soto Park is located, then went to Pinellas Point and Safety Harbor. DeSoto went on to explore much of the southeastern part of the United States, discovered the Mississippi River, but died a broken-hearted man because he didn't find the gold and silver he and the other Spaniards coveted so much. His death at the age of 42 had been foretold by an astrologer many years before.

It was DeSoto who started the postal service from St. Petersburg! While in this area, he wrote the first letter with a Florida dateline and sent it to the governor of Santiago, July 9, 1539.

In 1549, a tragedy occurred on the shores of Tampa Bay when the first white priest died on soil of the United States—Father Louis Cancer, who was massacred.

From time to time, other adventurers came this way. One of them was Capt. Pedro Menéndez, the intrepid founder of St. Augustine. He roamed both coasts of the state.

Though the Spaniards were to rule Florida for three centuries, very little more was done toward developing the West Coast section of the peninsula.

It is presumed that the Spanish influence was kept alive in this area by the few pioneer fishermen and farmers who may have migrated here from Cuba and Spain. The influence is borne out in the names of places, for instance. As a matter of fact, St. Petersburg is situated on Point Pinellas, originally called Punta Piñal, or "Point of the Pines." The names could have come from the early settlers, or may have even been handed down by the exploring map-makers of the early times.

No history of a community on the coast of Florida would be complete without mention of the pirates who marauded the region in the eighteenth century and on into the nineteenth. Over in Tampa, across the bay from St. Petersburg, the townspeople annually pay "tribute" to José Gaspar, who may actually be legendary, although there apparently were genuine pirates who plied these waters in the early days.

An old newspaper clipping has been preserved that gives us a glimpse of local color on piracy in these waters. A pioneer settler of the Pinellas peninsula was Mrs. Martha Anderson. She was interviewed on her 97th birthday anniversary and recorded her recollections of nearly a century of living in the region. She had actually known the wife of a pirate.

Here, then is an excerpt from the reporter's interview with Mrs. Anderson:

"Her tale of buried treasure...concerns the story of a sailor upon a ship besieged by pirates. All of the other sailors were slain and this particular one was taken ashore where he made his home with the pirate for years.

"The ship, which was scuttled and burned, lay on the beach at Long Key (near Pass-a-Grille) for many years. Its bulk with its massive chains will be remembered by old timers.

"Treasure taken from this ship, Mrs. Anderson says, was divided and buried in deep holes, covered over with sand over which was placed the body of a slain sailor and the whole carefully covered up. This precaution was taken so that, if the grave were discovered it would be thought to be just that and not be disturbed. One of these hiding places was thought to have been discovered by an English drifter who suddenly became wealthy without reason after visiting Long Key."

After the United States took over Florida in 1821, the Government carried on a long-running chase of the rogues of the sea and finally exterminated them. Part of the effort was the establishment of a network of lighthouses along the shorelines. The lighthouse on Egmont Key at the mouth of Tampa Bay dates back to 1848.

To an obscure pirate named Gómez goes the distinction of being the first publicity man for the Tampa Bay region. For it was this buccaneer who directed Dr. Odet Philippi to these parts by boasting of Tampa Bay, thusly: "If there is a God, surely this is His resting place. There is but one bay to compare with it, Naples…"

Dr. Philippi was the first white settler and grandfather of the first white child born in this region. He was directed here by Gómez in the 1830s. His grave is at Safety Harbor, overlooking Tampa Bay, which was known as Espiritu Santo Bay in the early times.

Dr. Philippi was a great-nephew of Louix XVI and friend and ex-schoolmate of Napoleon Bonaparte, who appointed him chief surgeon of the French armed forces. The British captured and imprisoned him in the Bahamas. He subsequently was freed after his heroic action in a yellow fever epidemic. He made his way over to South Carolina and joined the French Huguenots.

Philippi pulled stakes there in 1819, wound up in the Indian River region of Florida and was credited with originating the now famous Indian River citrus. Fearing an Indian uprising, he fled four years later. On the voyage his ship was intercepted by the pirates, who gave him the "Chamber of Commerce pitch" on Tampa Bay in return for the physician's medical services to the crew.

Dr. Philippi settled in the area, developing a huge plantation he called St. Helena, recognizing his friend Napoleon, who by then was in exile on St. Helena isle off Naples. The doctor cultivated a large grove, bringing the first grapefruit to Florida. It was destroyed in 1848 by a hurricane and tidal wave. During the Civil War, Dr. Philippi and his family moved to Hernando County for safety. They returned to their old plantation after the conflict.

In his sunset years, Dr. Philippi would sit by the waters he loved so very much and reflect on the past. He would say: "This is God's own country,

DR. ODET PHILLIPI was the first white settler in the Pinellas Peninsula and the grandfather of the first white child born in the region. (CNB)

and this water is His medicine, stirred by His hand, and deposited on this shore to heal man's suffering." He died in 1869.

For a brief period in the early 1840s, the Territory opened South Florida to homesteading. Only two dozen of these grants were made in what is now Pinellas County—and only three daring pioneers filed claims for the St. Petersburg area!

Rewarded for his services in the hot Seminole War was a Spaniard named Antonio Maximo Hernandez, who secured a land grant in 1843 and established a fish "rancho" at the lower end of the peninsula. The site of his operation became known as Maximo Point and remains so to this day. It is just off U.S. 19 as it approaches the Sunshine Skyway bridge. His fishery, which was for the supply of the Cuban market, was wiped out in the hurricane of 1848, and Maximo went back to Havana, where he died.

During the next 20 years or so, there was a scattering of a dozen or more "squatters," who endured the hardships of the frontier days.

For a colorful description of the typical pioneer life in Pinellas County, once again a newspaper clipping from the "Helen Huff Collection of Newspaper Clippings":

"Grandfather Cobb recalls his arrival in the Ridge section at the age of 19 years. His first job was driving range cattle for the magnificent pay of 50 cents a day. He was a good worker, so his pay later was raised to one dollar a day, big money for those days.

"Two years after his arrival he married. Then there was the problem of a home for himself and bride. Did he go to the mill for lumber, the supply company for other materials? No, for the simple reason there weren't any.

"So he built a log cabin, filling in the chinks between the logs with lime he manufactured in a home-made kiln. This is how it was done. He'd cart a load of oyster shells from the bay to the lime pit. Then above them he'd place a layer of firewood, then another layer of shells, another layer of wood, etc. Finally he'd set the whole thing on fire. The result: home-made lime. The bricks for the chimney was made by more or less the same process.

"Striking out for himself, Mr. Cobb raised cattle and cotton; yes, real cotton. He bought a tract of land for $1.25 an acre. His first cotton crop was a bumper one. He took it to Clearwater for marketing. And this was no simple process either. Nothing but sand roads; no hard surface, just sand, with deep ruts so difficult to travel that only a large-wheeled wagon would get on it. There were no bridges over the creeks and on several occasions he would have to wait a long time for the water to go down before he could cross without getting his load of cotton wet.

"Later Mr. Cobb turned to citrus raising. He says he planted or budded enough trees to supply a nation. A good percent of all the citrus trees in the ridge section were planted or budded by him.

HARDY PIONEERS to lower Pinellas Peninsula were Captain Abel Miranda and his wife Eliza, who came to Big Bayou in 1857 and settled there. They called him "the Rebel Terror of Tampa Bay." Miranda was a Minorcan whose family had first settled at St. Augustine. He was the brother-in-law of John Bethell, another Pinellas pioneer. The colorful Miranda was an Indian fighter, blockade runner, cattleman, and planter. His farm was attacked and ransacked by the Union forces during the Civil War. (Fuller)

"Mr. Cobb made very few trips to the cities in the old days. St. Petersburg was then nothing but a village with a very few scattered houses. Clearwater had a fort, a post office and a few houses. However, he found no need to go to the cities. Everything that was needed he raised himself."

Another pioneer about the time of Maximo was William Bunce, who had a "rancho" on Mullet Key, an area still known as "Bunce's Ranch" with a neighboring pass, known as Bunce's Pass. That big blow of 1848 ended the fishing business for Bunce as well as Maximo.

An early comer to the Point was Abel Miranda, who had fought in the Indian wars, and who moved from Tampa to Big Bayou. Here he homesteaded, built a home, and developed a fish rancho, thus reviving the fishing industry for this area. He was followed in 1859 by John T. Bethell, who moved to Little Bayou.

Tony Pizzo, author of the book *Tampa Town,* which traces the Latin families of the area, tells about Miranda's stay in Pinellas:

"The entire Point Pinellas was one vast wilderness, and 'full of game and varmints. That year I killed 11 bears and one panther; and ducks, wild geese and turkeys, I could get all I could make use of and never go a half mile from home.' Within a few years, he (Miranda) had made excellent progress in his fishing business, stock raising, truck farming and fruit culture. Miranda introduced the first alligator pear (avocado aguacate) in Florida. He had brought the seed from Cuba."

Miranda's prosperous farm and home was destroyed one day during the Civil War when the commandant of the Federal blockading fleet at Egmont Key ordered the estate wiped out. The troops raided it as well as setting it on fire. Miranda and his family fled to Tampa. He moved back to Pinellas after the war, purchasing a place several miles inland because he didn't want to chance another bombardment of his home from the sea.

After the war, a few settlers showed up in lower Pinellas. By 1876, a post office was established at Big Bayou or Disston City, near the present community of Gulfport. The post office was called Pinellas Village and John Bethell was the first postmaster. It was supplied by sailboats from Tampa and Cedar Key.

A real estate promotion called Disston City came into being, and in 1884 a town plat was recorded. It never prospered, however, and by the end of the decade it just faded away.

The beginning of St. Petersburg can be said to be the year 1875. By chance, an enterprising business man from Detroit, Mich.—he was Gen. John Constantine Williams, the "general" being an honorary title—visited Point Pinellas just as he was about to give up his search for a site for a new colony in Florida. His father was a pioneer resident of Detroit and served as the town's first mayor when it was incorporated in 1824. John C. Williams later was to hold several public positions in Detroit and he owned considerable property including an 80-acre farm on Woodward Avenue, four miles from the river.

General Williams came to Florida for his health. He was suffering from asthma and was ordered by his doctor to find a milder climate than Michigan. In 1875, he came down to Jacksonville, went up the St. Johns River, and visited Lake Okeechobee, Key West, Punta Rassa, Tampa, and Clearwater—but nothing suited him.

He was in Cedar Key, planning to return to Detroit, when a George W. Pratt of Chicago struck up a conversation with the General and suggested that he look at Point Pinellas.

"Damn Point Pinellas!" was Williams' strong reaction. "I was told by a gentleman from Tampa, also by one in Clearwater, that it is only four feet above tidewater!"

Pratt put the lie to that report, assuring the General that the area was 40 or 50 feet above sea level. Then he continued: "It is the healthiest and best section in the state of Florida. It is a perfect paradise, sir."

That did it. Williams retraced his steps to Clearwater, hired a team and journeyed to the Promised Land in South Pinellas County. He bought about 1,700 acres and in 1879 tried his hand at farming. This turned out to be a failure, and he went back North where he got a divorce and married again in 1892.

The General disposed of his property in Detroit and headed back south, coming to Tampa, where he built a home in the fashionable Hyde Park section. He continued his interest in St. Petersburg, however, and began negotiations with the promoters of a narrow gauge railroad, to be known as the Orange Belt Railroad, and to leave civilization at Sanford.

In the fall of 1887, the yellow fever epidemic struck Tampa. General Williams and his wife came to Pinellas peninsula to live. They lived at first at Big Bayou. The couple planned the new town together and, in 1891, General Williams

began construction of a showplace mansion at Fourth Street and Fifth Avenue South. But his health was failing, and in April, 1892, he passed away.

His death came as a blow to the community, as noted in this obituary:

"A pall of sadness envelopes the town! Its father, its benefactor, its far-seeing originator and friend is no more!...

"St. Petersburg, his idol, which his means rescued from the tangled wilderness and swamps of a few years ago, and which today is the most prosperous little town in the southern portion of the state, owes much to him, who, with such wisdom, guided her earliest years..."

Fortunately, however, Williams had lived to see his dream of a railroad reach what was to become bustling St. Petersburg.

In the little town of Longwood, near Sanford, there was a successful operator of a lumber business. He was Peter A. Demens, a Russian of noble ancestry, a political exile who had come to America to escape the tyranny of the Tsarist regime. The Russian form of his name was Piotr Alexeitch Demenscheff. Demens was a natural born promoter, a soldier of fortune, if you will. He was able to persuade Josef Henschen, a Swede; Henry Sweetapple, a Canadian, and A. M. Taylor, an American, to join him in 1885 in his idea of extending the railroad from Sanford to Pinellas Point.

A long and agonizing series of difficulties, mostly financial, plagued the builders of the Orange Belt. Construction gangs went off the job because of payless pay days. In one instance creditors went so far as to chain one of the locomotives to the rails until the company made good on its obligations. Nevertheless, the Road was completed, all 110 miles of it. On Monday, April 30, 1888, the first train chugged into its westermost terminal.

By the time the community had train service, it had a name of its own— St. Petersburg. The various promoters of the railroad had worked out names for post offices along the way. The Swede, Henschen, prodded by the postmistress for the little settlement, gave the town its name, honoring his partner Demens' home town back in Russia, St. Petersburg (now Leningrad).

"Why not call the town down there on the Gulf St. Petersburg," Henschen

[18]

WILLIAMS PARK originally was just called "City Park." The women of the town took an interest in it early, and some time in the late 1890s they raised money to build a fence around the park to keep out roaming cows. They also erected a bandstand. (Boyer)

mused, "it will never amount to much anyway, so its name won't make any difference!"

However, Demens' plan to make St. Petersburg the shipping capital of the South never materialized. The railroad failed to make money, and on Aug. 12, 1893, the Sanford and St. Petersburg Railway Co., owned by Henry B. Plant took over operation of the Orange Belt. In 1903 the Orange Belt Line was incorporated with the Atlantic Coast Line Railroad. It's now a part of the Seaboard Coast Line Railroad. In 1897, a standard gauge track was substituted for the old narrow gauge.

It is General Williams we may thank for the wide streets laid out many years ago, giving the city one of the best planned designs most anywhere. The General really was following the pattern set by Hamilton Disston, the saw and tool magnate from Philadelphia and one of the early developers of Florida (he brought four million acres of land from the State of Florida for 25 cents an acre!) who had put together Disston City (Gulfport). Disston had made his streets 100 feet wide; Williams could do no less. Later subdivisions followed the plan.

Not since the pirate touted Dr. Odet Philippe to the Tampa Bay region did the Pinellas peninsula get such a healthy boost as it did that day in the Spring of 1885 when a prominent physician stood before his colleagues at the national meeting of the American Medical Association and proclaimed the site of St. Petersburg as the healthiest spot on earth. This exposure just has to be the turning point in the early development of St. Petersburg. No publicity man could have pulled a more meaningful stunt to attract visitors and permanent residents than did this unsolicited testimonial from the medical world.

It seems that a decade earlier, in 1874, a London physician, Dr. B. W. Richardson, had suggested the establishment of a "Health City." Following

[19]

through on this suggestion, surveys were made of climatic conditions and other health factors. After long investigations, it was decided that Florida offered the best advantages, and observers were stationed in various parts of the state to see which was the best. One of the probers spent a year in Pinellas Point, and kept accurate records on the temperature, humidity, prevailing winds, amount of sunshine, and other health matters.

And then, on April 29 at the 36th annual meeting of the A.M.A., one of the most prominent physicians of the day, Dr. W. C. Van Bibber, of Baltimore, Md., read his paper. Some excerpts:

"Where should such a Health City be built? Overlooking the deep Gulf of Mexico, with the broad waters of a beautiful bay nearly surrounding it, with but little now upon its soil but the primal forest, there is a large sub-peninsula, Point Peninsula, waiting the hand of improvement.

"It lies in latitude 27 degrees and 42 minutes, and contains, with its adjoining keys, about 160,000 acres of land.

"No marsh surrounds its shores or rests upon its surface; the sweep of its beach is broad and graceful, stretching many miles, and may be improved to an imposing extent. Its average winter temperature is 72 degrees; that its climate is peculiar, its natural products show; that its air is healthy, the ruddy appearance of its few inhabitants attest.

"Those who have carefully surveyed the entire state, and have personally investigated this sub-peninsula and its surroundings, think that it offers the best climate in Florida. Here should be built such a city as Dr. Richardson has outlined."

The Van Bibber paper also contained this prophesy:

"It should be done at once, and when finished, invalids and pleasure-seekers, from all lands, will come to enjoy the delights of a winter climate, which, all things considered, can probably have no equal elsewhere."

This splendid speech stirred talk not only in the medical profession the world over, but among laymen as well. And it came to pass in later years that St. Petersburg, "The Sunshine City," did indeed become the world's Health City and mecca for "invalids and pleasure-seekers" as suggested by Dr. Van Bibber back in 1885.

As settlers began to move in, they became concerned about schooling for their youngsters. The first school session in St. Petersburg was held in a little wooden building erected in 1888 by the people of the city under the direction of the trustees of the Congregational Church. The first teacher was Miss Mamie Gilkeson, who resigned at the end of two months' service and was succeeded by Miss Olive Wickham. The building was located between Ninth and Tenth Streets near Central Avenue. Twenty nine pupils were enrolled in the first class.

As the era of the 1880s neared a close, other parts of Florida were enjoying the "tourist trade." St. Petersburg decided to get a piece of the action. So the new railroad began running "excursions" to the city, the first arriving on the Fourth of July in 1889. The entire town populace turned out to greet the visitors, who were delighted that peninsular Pinellas was cooler in the summer than the inland of the state.

A description of the way it was in St. Petersburg about this time comes from a Council Bluffs, Iowa, visitor, John A. Churchill, who years later told a newspaper reporter of his first visit in 1891:

"The only way you could get into the city by land was over the narrow-gauge Orange Belt Railway. The engine used to jump the track about once a week, but I never heard of any one being killed or even injured seriously—the train didn't go fast enough. Wood was used as fuel and, in wet weather, when the wood got wet, you could keep up with the train by walking.

"Fishing for Spanish mackerel on the railroad dock was great sport in those days and the market contained venison, wild turkey and Mallard ducks. The farmers brought in wagon loads of oranges and sold you a hatful for a nickel.

"Two large alligators made their home in the lake and basked in the sun on the shores undisturbed. Where some of the business buildings stand at present there were ponds. Good building lots could be had for $50 to $100 each. There were no paved streets or street lights at that time…"

There was some "progress" reported about this time. In 1889, a wooden sidewalk was started along Central Avenue at Ninth Street and built toward the bay. The community was responding to demands of the hardy pioneer women, who wanted a place to push their baby carriages.

St. Petersburg's "birth date" came on Leap Day—Feb. 29—in 1892, three years after it had come into existence. The local weekly newspaper, The *South Florida Home,* reported the event which took place in Cooper's Hall. The vote result was 15 for incorporation to 11 against, and, the newspaper observed: "St. Petersburg laid off her swaddling clothes and donned the more comely garb of an incorporated town."

There were two slates of officers proposed in the first election conducted that very day. The winning one was put up, the newspaper reported, by "the conservative, temperate, sturdy, working property owners, generally understood as the Anti-Saloon faction, and the other was put up by what was generally understood as the Open Saloon faction."

In the quaint style of reporting in that day, the newspaper pointed out that "The officers elected have the confidence of the entire community, and with the reins of government in their hands, a new era of faith and confidence in the future town is established.

"That the government will be conducted economically and with the best interests of every property owner in view, and also for the general good and prosperity of the town, every one feels assured."

Ironically the man who had founded St. Petersburg, the Detroit man who had the vision to see a great city ahead, General John C. Williams, went down to defeat in his bid for Mayor in that first election. By a better than two to one margin, David Moffett, who had come to the Point in 1881, overwhelmingly whipped the General. Sadly, less than two months after the election, General Williams died.

Ordinance No. 1, passed by the new city, "For the preservation of peace and morals in the town of St. Petersburg" provided that anyone caught violating the good order "by breach of peace, use of profanity, indecent exposure, disorderly conduct, or drunkenness," could be fined $100 or imprisoned up to 60 days.

The Council passed a closing law prohibiting sale of all merchandise (except drugs or other "necessaries of life") on the Sabbath Day, with a penalty of $5 to $100 fine or up to 25 days imprisonment.

Another early ordinance outlawed hogs running at large inside the city and gave the town marshal the power to impound the animals and to auction them off if the owners didn't settle up with the city.

A law set a speed limit for trains or engines of six miles per hour through the city, and it outlawed reckless driving or racing of horses or teams.

The beginning of the new century found St. Petersburg which became a city by charter in 1903 on the move. The town government was issuing bonds for public improvements. The electric light plant, operated by F. A. Davis, formerly of Philadelphia, began operations in 1897, and in 1902, Bell Telephone Co. completed its Tampa line and the people of St. Petersburg could call across the bay for a toll of 25 cents.

Everything was not coming up roses, however. In 1902, the St. Petersburg State Bank, which had been organized in 1892, folded and irate depositors were in the mood to lynch the president.

Ecologists and nature-lovers became upset because a group of men in the lower peninsula were killing birds for their plumes, feathers, and eggs.

John A. Bethell, historian of that period, reported "one season they got 11,000 skins and plumes, 30,000 birds' eggs, and with a force of 11 men with blowpipes, it was impossible to blow the contents out of more than half of these eggs before they were spoiled. Then they had to peck holes in the ends of the balance and spread them out over the face of creation for the ants to do the rest. That was the greatest destruction of the feathered tribe at any time."

This wanton destruction in the 1890s had been witnessed by Roy L. Hanna, a St. Petersburg resident. In one day he saw the destruction of three bushels of pelican, cormorant, and crane eggs. Hanna thought up the idea of a sanctuary. So he took steps to buy a small island, Indian Key, which belonged to the State of Florida. In 1902 he learned that the Federal government wanted the island as a bird reservation. He corresponded personally with President Theodore

[22]

Roosevelt and turned over all his rights to the island—which is now appropriately called Bird Key, and is just off Maximo Point.

Later, at the request of Hanna and his co-founder of the St. Petersbrug Audubon Society, Mrs. Katherine Bell Tippetts, the islands known as Cow, Calf and Bush, were made parts of Bird Key by executive order of President Warren G. Harding.

Tourism got a big boost in 1909 when on November 16 the first through Pullman from New York City arrived in St. Petersburg over the A.C.L. The excited community was alerted to the possibilities by the local newspapers which prophesied: "In a few years, many through Pullmans will be coming into St. Petersburg each day from the North, bringing hundreds of tourists. St. Petersburg is now on the threshold of its greatest development."

St. Petersburg became truly "The Sunshine City" on Sept. 1, 1910, when the publisher of the evening newspaper, *The Independent,* Lew B. Brown, announced to the world a sensational offer: He promised to give away all copies of his newspaper every day the sun didn't shine on St. Petersburg!

In a full page display ad in his paper that day, Brown proclaimed the good news:

"Government records prove that the nearest approach to perpetual sunshine to be found in the whole United States is at 'St. Petersburg by the Gulf Stream,' 'St. Petersburg the Beautiful,' 'St. Petersburg the Home of Perpetual Summer,' 'St. Petersburg the Riviera of the Sunny South,' 'St. Petersburg the Flag Bearer of Growth and Prosperity.'

"To Prove our Faith: In the recurrence daily of gladsome sunshine throughout the fall and winter, when all is cloud and gloom in the Northland, the EVENING INDEPENDENT challenges the world by inaugurating today a standing offer to give away—ABSOLUTELY FREE—WITHOUT COST OR CONDITION—to subscribers and strangers alike—at the office, or on the carrier routes or on the streets—FREE FREE FREE THE EVENING INDEPENDENT free every day the sun doesn't shine on St. Petersburg...

"Remember, there is no condition. It is done for no other reason than to prove to all men that the days when we do not enjoy sunshine must be few—else The Independent could not afford to make such a reckless offer. It is the only newspaper in the whole United States which DARES to make such an offer. We challenge them all..."

The Independent had been purchased on December 15, 1908, by Brown from Willis B. Powell. He died in 1944 and the afternoon paper was sold by his son and publisher-successor, L. Chauncey Brown, to Ralph Nicholson of *The Tampa Daily Times* in 1951. It later was sold to Canadian publishing magnate, Roy Thomson, who finally sold it to its long-time competitor, the morning *St. Petersburg Times.*

The Independent's "Sunshine Offer" is still in effect and in the more than

60 years since it was first made the paper has been given away on an average of fewer than four times per year. One of the longest streaks of sunny days, during which the paper did not have to make good its offer, was a 764-day string ended March 17, 1969.

In 1910, St. Petersburg officials were wrestling with moral problems. Some Protestant ministers sought to make the town a "model city." They passed a resolution against the evils of card playing, dancing, intoxication, and cigaret smoking. They said: "We deplore the increasing use of tobacco and cigarets by our youth and children, believing that the use of tobacco in any form is unnecessary, expensive and harmful . . . We ask that the sign on a cigar store on Central Avenue, which is considered disgraceful and blasphemous, reading 'You had better smoke here than hereafter,' be removed by the Council or public protest."

That was in February. By November of 1910, under pressure of Blue Sunday advocates, the City Council passed an ordinance prohibiting the sale of all kinds of merchandise on Sundays, except the prescriptions ordered by physicians of the city. A facetious newsman observed: "This will be a severe blow to the people who are compelled to purchase their meals on Sunday, as they will have to eat enough Saturday night to last until Monday morning." The ordinance was short-lived; the following meeting, the Council repealed it by a vote of four to one.

Sparsely-settled Gulfport became an incorporated town in 1910, amid complaints from the land owners and others that it would be a costly experiment. The *St. Petersburg Times* editorialized:

"Gulfport is perhaps the largest town in Florida, territorially speaking, and for population per square mile it is undoubtedly the largest on earth—and for good hard American cheek it perhaps will compare with any in the country, the taking in of large areas of valuable lands that can never receive any benefits of the corporation whatsoever and are taken only to be taxed, being nothing more nor less than a hold-up..."

The editor of *The Times* in those days was W. L. Straub, who had come down from the cold of North Dakota in 1900 and soon acquired the weekly *West Hillsborough Times* (Pinellas was then still part of Hillsborough County), which had been founded in 1884.

Through the years, dating as far back as 1886, there had been agitation to divide Pinellas from the apron strings of "Mother Hillsborough." The main complaint the west coast residents had had against their Tampa-dominated county government was the inattention and neglect in providing decent roads and bridges to serve the near water-locked Point of Pines peninsula.

A trip by train was a long, tiresome, roundabout journey covering 160 miles and two changes, way up to Trilby, south to Lakeland and then west to Tampa. It took a full day of travel. And because of poor roads, a drive by automobile was next to impossible. The chief mode of travel was by boat, but due to schedules it was not always possible to make the round trip in one day.

The gauntlet for division was flung down by Straub in a hot editorial in the *St. Petersburg Times* on February 23, 1907. It was, indeed, a "Pinellas Declaration of Independence." Editor Straub took a poke at Tampa's crime record, commenting:

"The writer intends no criticism of Tampa and its people here. All good citizens of the West Coast are proud of Tampa as one of the South's great cities. But it is a simple fact that the big city of Tampa—as with all big cities— in many ways causes for the county very heavy expenses—notably through the criminal records of the big city—nine murder cases at one court session, for instance—that such a community as ours of the West Coast has little or no part in, except to help pay the bills..."

A skillful maneuver in the 1911 session of the Florida Legislature resulted in a law creating Pinellas subject to a referendum set for November 14 of the same year. The vote result was 1,379 "for" and 505 "against," which was 248 more than the necessary three-fifths vote required by the legislative bill in a severe test of the faith of the Pinellas residents in the strength of their cause.

The campaign leading up to the election had been heated. Straub was swapping editorial insults daily with editor E. D. Lambright of *The Tampa Morning Tribune* and editor D. B. McKay of *The Tampa Daily Times,* who was also the mayor of Tampa. Supporting Straub was E. L. Pearce, the mayor of Clearwater and editor of the *Clearwater News,* as well as editor Lew Brown of the *St. Petersburg Independent.*

No sooner had the division issue been settled when a newer and even hotter spat developed. St. Petersburg politicians wanted their city to be the county seat for the new county, Pinellas; Clearwater wanted their city to be the county seat.

The legislative act had made Clearwater the county seat, and the *St. Petersburg Times* reported the arrangement had the approval of 90 percent of the people of St. Petersburg.

Years later, in recalling the squabble, Straub related "There were some here (St. Petersburg) we called 'Sooners,' who did not agree and were all the time determined on a court house raid at the first chance. And Clearwater's political populace being of that kind which trust nobody, after January 1 (1912) trouble came promptly and plenteously.

"It all started when clever Clearwater politicians, aided and abetted by some politically foolish citizens of St. Petersburg put over a politically crooked deal in the first county election and captured for Clearwater, or the 'up-county,' a three-to-two control of the Board of County Commissioners, and gerrymandered the newly formed districts to perpetuate the control—and so well done it was that it stands today (1939) as invincible as ever."

Fearing that the "Sooners" and other south county folk would try and steal the county site away from them, the Clearwater people set about to build a court house as quickly as possible to seal their coup.

"So the Big Three (County Commissioners) got a bunch of the boys together and built a court house one Sunday instead of going to church," the *St. Petersburg Times* editor added.

The lumber used to build the courthouse was sawed in Tampa and each piece numbered so the unskilled volunteer laborers could erect it. The material was hauled to the site by mule team. The structure was put together almost overnight by torchlight. Neighbor women did their part by cooking food and bringing it to the amateur carpenters. One report is that the court house was built so quickly they forgot to include toilets.

At night armed citizens patrolled all sides of the building during the construction because rumors had been spread that St. Petersburg citizens might try to burn it down, so deep was the feeling over the county seat.

St. Petersburg turned out to be an ideal site for Spring training for major league baseball, but its possibility as such was not realized until 1913. The first pro team to discover Florida was the Washington Nationals which way back in 1888 put in a stint at Jacksonville.

But it was St. Petersburg a quarter of a century later that really gave Spring training under clear skies and warm temperatures a boost. Civic-minded citizens formed a baseball association in the summer of 1913, and capitalized it at $10,000. Subsequently the amount was increased to $50,000, raised by popular subscription.

On September 19 that year of 1913, the owner and president of the St. Louis Browns came down to St. Petersburg, looked over the site, liked what he saw—and signed the contract the very next day. The local committee agreed to pay total expenses of the team while it was in training.

Thus in the Spring of 1914, St. Petersburg had big league baseball. The first game was played February 27. More than 4,000 fans saw the Browns lose to the Chicago Cubs that day, with a score of 3 to 2. The Cubs, then training in Tampa, made the trip to St. Petersburg via steamboat—trains and causeways were too slow!

A few years before this, in 1909, a former Pittsburgh laundry operator, Al F. Lang, had come to the Sunshine City for his health. He became prominent in local affairs and in 1914 was elected mayor. He was an ardent baseball fan and a friend of top club officials. Through his efforts, the Philadelphia Phillies came here for training in 1915. The team went back north for the regular season—and won 14 of the first 15 games played, with St. Petersburg getting much of the credit for this splendid record because of the fine weather it offered the players during spring training.

[26]

Through the years, springtime baseball has offered first class entertainment to the tourists and home folks alike. Probably the most popular player of all time, who thrilled the crowds with his home runs, was Babe Ruth who came to St. Petersburg with the New York Yankees in 1925.

St. Petersburg honored Al Lang for his role in the baseball program by naming the training base Al Lang Field.

About the time baseball came to the Sunshine City other entertainment was on the bill. George S. Gandy in 1912 had acquired the corner of Central Avenue and Fifth Street and built what at first was referred to as "Gandy's White Elephant." What it was was a theatre, known as the Plaza, along with a hotel and office buildings.

The Plaza opened on the evening of Monday, March 8, 1913, with Cammaranos' "Il Trovatore," played by the Royal Italian Company. Gandy, who had moved down from Philadelphia where he had been prominent in the transportation field, paid $34,000 for the site of his "White Elephant," then he poured $125,000 into an imposing Spanish-Style structure boasting the largest stage south of Atlanta.

All the big stars showed up at the Plaza at one time or another. There were Sophie Tucker, Burns and Allen, Geraldine Farrar, Madame Schumann-Heink, Ruth St. Dennis. Also there were Ted Shawn, Pavlova, John Philip Sousa's Band, the mighty orator William Jennings Bryan, the George White "Scandals" and Earl Carroll's "Vanities." Any place that can book such spectacular talent can't be all "white elephant."

As St. Petersburg entered the teens, it was just emerging from a sleepy village to a lively town. A glimpse of how it was in 1912 comes from an eye-witness, Arthur W. Calhoun, who recently wrote *The Times* about it:

"...Transit was adequate: During the season four trains a day each way on the Atlantic Coast Line, and three steamboats daily each way between Tampa and Bradenton. Street cars from 9th St. and 7th Ave. N., via downtown to Veteran City (now Gulfport) gave easy access to Boca Ceiga Bay, then unspoiled, and a launch ran to Pass-a-Grille.

"The school system was admittedly the best in the state, and tourists could bring their children without damage to their year's schooling, even if they arrived in November and left in March.

"A three-week midwinter Chautauqua brought notable talent in music and lecture.

"In 1910 the city was alive from February through August with a mass meeting every Friday in the park on behalf of the campaign to ratify the state Prohibition Amendment. Both papers gave ample coverage. Even then, the *Independent* was a lively daily. The *Times* came twice a week.

"Fresh from Pittsburgh, I did not find Pinellas sleepy. I awoke."

St. Petersburg made history when commercial aviation was born right here on the bright, beautiful New Year's morn of 1914.

An intrepid pilot named Tony Jannus lifted his Benoist airboat off the waters of the Yacht Basin in St. Petersburg, and began a historic flight over the bay to Tampa. Jannus and his lone passenger, A. C. Pheil, who had paid $400 in a bid to have the honor, landed at the foot of Lee Street on Hillsborough River in Tampa 23 minutes later.

A reporter on the scene of the takeoff wrote: "An immense crowd watched the first flight of the air boat, every pier and the sea wall being crowded. Jannus made his start from the north of the breakwater at the entrance to the yacht basin. The crowd yelled as the pilot gave the signal to shove off and, with the propeller whirling at high speed, he took the water, the engine sounding like a score of machine guns. The boat headed west and skimmed across the yacht basin, making a turn in front of the Home Line docks."

Jannus skipped along at 50 feet above water most of the way, but upon approaching Tampa he lifted the craft to about 150 feet "so as to give his passenger a better view of the city which must have been a beautiful one indeed," the reporter wrote. He added "Jannus can go even higher if he chooses." A cheering crowd of some 3,000 persons were on hand to greet the first commercial flight. Ex-mayor Pheil scampered from the plane the moment it touched down, quickly ran to a telephone to call home and let the folks know he made the journey safely.

The St. Petersburg-Tampa Airboat Line, as it was known, continued on regular scehdule. The first parcel flown contained photos from the *St. Petersburg Times* addressed to the Tri-Color Engraving Co. in Tampa. They were due to be flown back the next day, but Jannus' plane capsized in the bay and the engravings were shipped by train. The first express package sent was a Swift & Co. premium ham, and the firm took out a full page ad in *Colliers* magazine to brag about a "first."

By March 17, 1914, the record was 1200 passengers without an accident. After the publicity died down, business dropped, and the service was discontinued. Jannus later flew for the Russian Aero Service and was killed in a crash in 1916. His brother Rodger, also a pilot, was killed nearly two years later while in the Air Service during World War I in France.

A local historian once wrote that while Al Lang was mayor, "St. Petersburg emerged from the village class and became a full-fledged city, and Mr. Lang helped materially in this change."

A lot of things did happen while the erstwhile Pennsylvanian was chief executive. He first was elected in 1914 and was reelected in 1916 for another two year term. The part he played in bringing big league baseball to the Suncoast has already been recorded here. But there were other achievements.

Lang succeeded in having push carts and peanut wagons barred from

Central Avenue. Then he went about clearing the jungle of signs and bill-boards, kicking off the drive with one grand "Sign Pulling Down Day," getting rid of all hanging signs.

And it was while Lang was mayor that St. Petersburg adopted an ordinance that standarized the benches in shape and size and established *green* as the *only* color the benches could be painted. This was the beginning of the image of St. Petersburg as the green bench city, a projection the community later tried to get away from. The story of the benches begins back in 1907 when Noel Mitchell was mayor. He had a real estate office at Fourth and Central. His ground floor offices became the hangout for idle tourists who appreciated his comfortable chairs. But the office became too crowded to work in. Thus Mitchell came up with the idea of constructing comfortable benches on the wide sidewalks. Other merchants followed suit. They became a trademark of this haven for winter visitors. Incidentally, Mitchell's benches were painted a bright orange!

Late in the 1960s the city fathers decided that the benches were nice, but their somber color wasn't good, and that St. Petersburg should do something to get away from the image of being just a haven for senior citizens. So the City Council decreed new resting places must be of aluminum tubing and natural finish wooden slates of either Douglas fir or clear heart redwood "dressed, free of knots and splinters." And that was that. The deadline for compliance was August of 1969.

Another St. Petersburg institution—the famed Festival of States—came into being while Al Lang was mayor. Actually, the pageant was an offshoot of a childrens' parade that began in 1896—a march on Washington's Birthday. This was a colorful event in those formative years of the community. Subsequently, the festival idea went through several metamorphoses as a fair, an exhibition, a tourist fair and, in 1914, a DeSoto celebration. Then it was discontinued for a period, the schools feeling that the Washington parade took too much time of the children.

The community celebration was started again, though, in 1917 when Captain William Neal, scout for the Philadelphia National Baseball Club, came to town and proposed a festivity such as Mardi Gras as part of the hoopdela for spring training. Neal worked then with Mayor Lang and developed a week of parades and dances and other activities—all saluting the states where St. Petersburg's "crop" of tourists came from.

The big show was omitted during the World War I years but resumed in 1922. It is still going strong (although the string of events was broken once again by World War II and the Festival discontinued). And every year the sponsors and spectators get the feeling it is "bigger and better" than ever.

A war and a disaster marred the time as the dizzying Twenties approached and began. As did communities throughout the country, St. Petersburg felt

[29]

the effects of World War I. Numerous young men were called into service, and the home folks supported the war effort in many ways.

And then one day in October of 1921, the West Coast felt the deadly punch of a tropical hurricane. L. Chauncey Brown, former publisher of *The Evening Independent* who established the city's first weather station in 1914, has been quoted as saying the 1921 hurricane was "decidedly the worst I ever saw here." Brown came to St. Petersburg in 1910.

Disaster struck on October 25. At 2 P.M. the barometer fell to 28.81, wind gusts reached 100 miles an hour, and 6.48 inches of rain fell in a 24 hour period. The water rose to 10.5 feet above mean low tide, five feet higher than in any other hurricane since 1848. Ships were washed as far as half a mile inland.

The storm roared in from the western Caribbean, swirled around Cuba, zoomed upward through the Gulf and made landfall about Tarpon Springs. This, of course, put St. Petersburg on the strong side of the blow.

The word spread that Pass-a-Grille had been "wiped out." But the fears were dispelled when at the height of the hurricane, the *St. Petersburg Times* published its famed "Motorcycle Extra" assuring the world that no lives were lost at Pass-a-Grille, although property loss was heavy. The *Times,* elated over the happy news, chirped: "Wild reports were circulated by other publications that 90 persons had perished."

The "Motorcycle Extra" got its name from the fact the *Times* borrowed a two-cylinder Indian motorcyle, attached a belt from its rear wheel to the linotype machine and cranked out the newspapers that way. The "extra" which kept the *Times* record of never missing and edition was printed on an old flat-bed press.

The 1921 hurricane was just an interlude to the big happenings of the decade of the Roarin' Twenties. All of Florida became a spectacular real estate boom, but it seems that St. Petersburg was one of the very first of the resort cities to get the ball rolling.

As the versatile Ford automobile, the Model-T, came into the reach of more and more Americans, the open road called to the warm clime and beautiful towns and countryside of Florida. The tourists truly discovered St. Petersburg, and the winter of 1920-21 saw them converge here in record numbers. So much so that there was the problem of accommodating the nomads.

Noel A. Mitchell, then mayor of the city, came up with the bright idea of establishing a Tent City. Up went scores and scores of tents on a city-owned block at 18th Street and Second Avenue South. Soon hundreds of families were using the facilities. Those were the days of the "Tin Can Tourists," and many of them had their own tents and camping equipment.

This phenomenon, according to Walter P. Fuller, was the beginning of the dizzying Florida real estate boom, though no one recognized it as such at the moment.

[30]

The 1920 census gave St. Petersburg a population of 14,237, which was about 14,000 more than the city had in the 1890 census. By 1925, at the height of the boom, the population swelled to 50,000!

The boom days were zany, but St. Petersburg was making hay while its brilliant sun shone. In 1926, there was a book called *"Florida in the Making,"* written by Frank Parker Stockbridge and John H. Perry, the latter being a newspaper and radio tycoon in Florida for decades. The authors commended this community for its truth in advertising.

"It (St. Petersburg) might as appropriately be nicknamed 'The City that Advertising Built,'" wrote Stockbridge and Perry, "for there is no other community in all Florida in which the united efforts of the entire citizenship have been so acutely and intelligently concentrated upon advertising its advantages. The St. Petersburg Chamber of Commerce has been the pacemaker for the rest of Florida in this respect. It was the St. Petersburg Advertising Club, under the presidency of William C. Freeman, which started, in the early months of 1925, the movement to remove from Florida the stigma of misleading advertising and fraudulent promotions, and the St. Petersburg *Daily News,* the newspaper founded by Frank F. Pulver, a former mayor of the city, has taken an advanced position in the campaign to protect the good name of Florida against unscrupulous and irresponsible attacks and representations."

Another writer of the day, Frederick Lewis Allen, who reported on the Twenties, mentioned some of the goofy advertising that took place in some other parts of Florida. "'Manhattan Estates,'" he wrote, "was advertised as being 'not more than three-fourths of a mile from the prosperous and fast-growing city of Nettie'; there was no such city as Nettie, the name being that of an abandoned turpentine camp, yet people bought."

It was the famed bachelor, Pulver, when he was mayor, who created such a stir in New York City during the boom times. City publicist John Lodwick was one of the best in his business. Walter Fuller tells in his book *St. Petersburg and Its People* that Lodwick's "masterpiece was the colorful, photogenic 'millionaire bachelor' mayor, Frank Fortune Pulver, who one day strolled down Broadway in New York City, attired from head to foot in white and attended by several beauty queens. This stunt caused an historic traffic jam."

The enterprising business community of St. Petersburg quickly reacted to the need of fine hotel facilities. Ten big hotels were erected between the days of Tent City in 1920 and the height of the boom in 1925. They were, in order of completion, the Soreno, Pheil, Suwannee, Mason (now Princess Martha), Pennsylvania, Dennis, Vinoy Park, Jungle, Rolyat, and Don Cesar.

New roads, streets, and subdivisions were laid out. City limits were moved to the tip of the peninsula. Bridges were extended to the Gulf Beaches, municipal parks opened, and the entire Tampa Bay waterfront was secured for public use.

A significant engineering feat was accomplished when the Gandy Bridge toll span between St. Petersburg and Tampa was opened on November 20, 1924. "The bridge is built!" exclaimed the builder, George S. (Dad) Gandy, who had pursued the project for more than 20 years. After many setbacks and disappointments, Gandy "went public" in 1922 and enlisted the services of Eugene M. Elliott, a colorful promoter who with a crew of super-salesmen conducted a razzle-dazzle campaign and sold $2 million worth of preferred stock in 122 days!

In the other direction, a ferry was established across the Bay to Bradenton in 1924.

About this time, St. Petersburg hustled to complete a landmark unique to the city: The "Million Dollar Pier." The first St. Petersburg pier was erected with the coming of the train in 1888. And in 1920, a $40,000 bond issue paid for a new pier—but this span was wiped out in the vicious 1921 hurricane. At the height of the boom, in 1925, the city taxpayers approved the million-dollar bond issue to build a new pier which remained popular through the years. The pier was replaced with a new structure that opened in 1972.

A most unusual institution was born in St. Petersburg in 1925. "Doc" Webb opened his drug store here that year. J. E. Webb, a native of Nashville, Tenn., with a flair for salesmanship and promotion and color, started his little 17-by-28-foot drug store which was to become "The World's Most Unusual Drug Store." It has grown continuously since the day he opened its doors and today there are 77 stores in a single shopping area. "Doc" had started the firm with a $5,000 nest egg he had saved from his job in Nashville.

An educational institution of note came into being in 1927. It was the St. Petersburg Junior College, still going strong, although now under a new name, St. Petersburg Community College.

After the boom came the bust. When the great national depression closed in, St. Petersburg was still reeling from the real estate debacle of the mid-20s. All of its nine banks had collapsed; only three of 18 remained open in Pinellas County. Script was being used instead of money, and by 1930 some 10,000 people had moved out, dropping the population back to 40,000. There were no jobs here. Relief programs kept the unemployed busy working on weed gangs at $1 a day. Collection of City taxes was off 52 percent.

Things got so bad that a sign at the city limits cautioned newcomers who might have the idea of coming here to live!

Despite conditions, life went on, new ventures began. The depression years brought other important improvements. A new City Charter of council-manager type government was drawn up in 1931, and a City Civil Service system from employees was instituted.

Another important facility, the Bay Pines Veteran Hospital opened on an 800-acre tract in 1933. It was an ornate Spanish style building that cost about $1 million.

In 1933, a group of business men, headed by Raleigh W. Greene Sr., put together the First Federal Savings & Loan Association, now housed in the "Big Blue" building that dominates downtown.

In the depth of the Big Depression, on the morning of Oct. 15, 1934, a single-engine monoplane took off from Albert Whitted Airport, thus launching National Airlines, which was to become one of the great airlines of the nation. Stocky, dynamic George T. (Ted) Baker, one-time barnstormer from Northern Illinois, arrived in Florida with two planes and a figurative shoestring. He won an airmail contract from the U.S. Post Office Department to fly the mail on the 150-mile route between St. Petersburg and Daytona Beach. With that contract, four associates, $2,000 capital, and boundless energy. *The Miami News* once recalled, Ted Baker began operations. The miniature airline during that year carried mail and 400 passengers and Baker began to expand— Miami, Sarasota, Fort Myers. Eventually, he got the lucrative Miami-New York route.

As 1940 decade began, St. Petersburg was beginning to emerge from the nightmare of the economic depression, but soon faced World War II. The community was almost totally tourist-oriented, and the town began to suffer when the number of visitors on wheels declined because of gasoline rationing and other restrictions.

Fortunately, the armed forces moved into this vacuum. The U.S. Air Corps decided to use St. Petersburg as a major training site for recruits and began to requisition plush resort hotels to house the boys. The fancy Vinoy Park was taken over first, then 58 other resort hotels were turned into troop barracks, including the big Don-Cesar on St. Petersburg Beach. Only the Suwannee downtown was left a civilian hotel. A tent city went up on the golf course at the Jungle Hotel to handle the additional thousands of troops assigned to duty here.

St. Petersburg became the home for many airmen stationed at Tampa's giant MacDill Field across the bay. Also, MacDill personnel flocked to the Gulf coast beaches on leave time. Thus the stage was set for the Federal government to take over Gandy Bridge and the Davis Causeway between Tampa and Clearwater, both toll facilities. Claude Pepper, U.S. Senator in 1944, was in a hot race for reelection. He prevailed upon his close friend, President Franklin D. Roosevelt, to apply Federal muscle to take over and free the spans under wartime powers. Pepper was reelected.

In the post-World War II years, St. Petersburg resumed normal living and carried on many public improvements to meet demands of a growing population.

Stetson University in DeLand moved its law school to Gulfport, taking over the old Rolyat Hotel. The University of South Florida opened its Bay campus here.

Gandy Bridge got a twin span to double-lane the facility. A new trans-Bay bridge was built midway between the Gandy and Davis spans, the Howard Frankland Bridge which was to become part of the Interstate system. The Sunshine Skyway bridge between St. Petersburg and Bradenton was built and subsequently four-laned. U.S. 19 was brought across the city, and now Interstate 75 is providing a cross-city expressway, linking to the Sunshine Skyway. The county also completed the Bayway, a 15-mile bridge and causeway connection between St. Petersburg and St. Petersburg Beach and Fort DeSoto Park on Mullet Key.

In 1953, St. Petersburg brought the first television to the Bay area when the City-owned WSUN-TV went on the air.

There was a lot of action on the political front after World War II, with the Republicans becoming the controlling party. Early in the 1950s the area sent a young lawyer, William C. Cramer, to Congress, the first Republican to represent the state in Congress since the Reconstruction days. He remained in office many terms. In the late 1960s, a St. Petersburg man, Ray C. Osborne, became the first Lieutenant Governor of the state in this century, with the reestablishment of that office.

In 1963, the *St. Petersburg Times* won journalism's most coveted award, the Pulitzer prize. An investigative team, headed by reporter Martin Waldron, now with *The New York Times,* exposed shenanigans in the construction and operation of the Florida Turnpike.

Florida Presbyterian College began classes in the fall of 1960. In 1971, Jack Eckerd, drug store magnate, philanthropist and unsuccessful candidate for Governor, gave Florida Presbyterian a gift of $10 million, for a total of contributions of $12.5 million—and the name of the institution was changed to Eckerd College.

Building continued throughout the city and area. The newest town hotel was the new Hilton, a skyscraper.

Ranking second smallest in land area among Florida's 67 counties—only Union (Lake Butler) is smaller—Pinellas has only 264 square miles, or about 166,400 acres. Yet, it is the most heavily populated, and estimates give it the ratio of 1,800 persons per square mile. Pinellas County is the only Florida county occupying an entire subpeninsula. For this reason, it is often called "Little Florida."

In the Spring of 1973 came the good news that St. Petersburg had been named an All-American City, a much sought after award of the National Municipal League and the *Saturday Evening Post.*

The lead on the banner story in the *St. Petersburg Times* told the story in a nutshell:

"St. Petersburg, a city divided by strikes and violence in 1968 but working in 1972 to solve critical problems of growth, environment, race and social conditions, has been named an All-American City…"

[34]

St. Petersburg before 1900

LOOKING LIKE A WESTERN TOWN, this was St. Petersburg in 1887 prior to the coming of the railroad. It was about this time that St. Petersburg got its name, from the town back in Russia whence came Peter A. Demens, who soon was to bring the Orange Belt Railroad here. (CNB)

FIRST POSTMASTER of St. Petersburg was a pioneer merchant, E. R. Ward. He built one of the first residence in the community, seen here in the foreground with horses and wagons in front. The post office was established in 1888 in Ward's general store on Ninth Street. The first letter with St. Petersburg in the address was received by Ed T. Lewis. Prior to this time, Pinellas Village and Bonifacio were the only settlements with postal facilities. Ward also was instrumental in starting an early school in the town. (Boyer)

OLDEST CHURCH in St. Petersburg is St. Bartholomew's Episcopal Church, organized April 20, 1887, when the town was but a budding village without even a railroad. The original church was on the corner of Lakeview Avenue and 19th Street South. It was built of heart pine, of Florida Gothic design, and its dimensions were 18 feet by 40 foot. The church was enlarged five times at this location, and each time the original building was incorporated into the new structure. The real estate was donated by Dr. and Mrs. John B. Abercrombie. Church records show that $246 for the church was raised in America, $383 in England, and $44 at a bazaar held by the church members. (CNB)

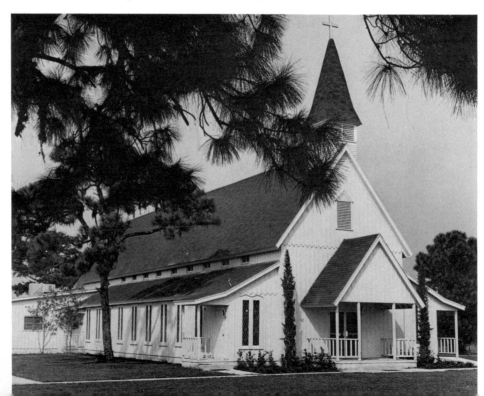

THE RAILROAD was brought to St. Petersburg by Piotr Alexeitch Demenscheff—or Peter A. Demens—when the first locomotive of the Orange Belt Railroad chugged into the city pulling cars on April 20, 1888. Demens was a Russian of noble ancestry, a political exile, who had come to America to escape the tyranny of the Tsarist regime. He was a successful operator of a lumber business at Longwood, near Sanford, before he got into the railroad business. (Fuller)

ITS MERITS WERE FEW and its shortcomings many and obvious, someone has said of the old Orange Belt Railroad which linked St. Petersburg with the interior of Florida before the turn of the century. Above, the crew of one of the early locomotives pose proudly beside the iron horse. (PCHC)

The Orange Belt survived just long enough to "break its backers, and give birth to a village and a dream." The primitive transportation system was acquired by the Plant System which later became the Atlantic Coast Line. The photo below has been identified as the first ACL locomotive to come into the city after the firm took over. The name "Orange Belt" had been changed to "Tampa and Gulf Coast" and then to "Atlantic Coast Line." (Boyer)

[37]

THE RAILROAD PIER at the end of First Avenue South was an early landmark and a proud contribution to the city from Peter Demens. It was the railroad owner's dream that some day St. Petersburg would be a deep harbor port, and his pier was a salute in that direction. This is a view of it in 1889.

Steamers and sailing vessels called at the pier, and fishermen went about the business and fun of catching the whoppers as this picture proves. The steamers included the *H. B. Plant* and the *Margaret* which brought mail and freight and picnic parties from Tampa. (Boyer)

END OF THE PIER *(above)* was a popular spot in the early days and fishermen angled for the big ones. The pier was a forerunner of the popular piers that have succeeded it to this day.

 H. W. Hibbs built a thriving fish house at the end of the pier *(below),* where he advertised "fresh fish daily," oysters, and ice. The bathing pavilion is at the right. (Boyer)

THIS UNIQUE SAIL CAR was the idea of Henry Hibbs, the owner of the ice plant at the end of the pier. Hibbs had been unable to get a steam engine to haul his ice from the Crystal Ice Co. in town to the fish packing houses at the end of the pier. He rigged up a mast on a flatcar, mounted a leg-of-mutton sail, and used the breeze to propel the vehicle. It was Florida's first and only sail train. Old timers said that strangers, seeing the "train" sailing through the streets almost decided to join the anti-saloon league. (Green)

CENTER OF SOCIAL ACTIVITY was the bathing-dancing pavillion built on the pier by D. S. Brantley, grandfather of former St. Petersburg Mayor Ed Brantley. It was built in 1890 and featured fresh water showers from an artesian well, and a toboggan slide was added in 1891. On weekends, this was a swinging place, for the steamboats brought excursionists over from Tampa. (CNB)

CENTRAL AVENUE, now St. Petersburg's main street, has been popular since the beginning of the city. But in 1895, when this picture was taken looking east, the street was deep sand which made it rather rugged pulling for horses and wagons. Sign on the building at right advertised Martin's Pharmacy and announced that a "blood purifier and tonic" was made there. (Boyer)

THE DETROIT HOTEL has been a landmark in St. Petersburg since its construction in 1888. It was a joint venture of the town's founders, Peter Demens and General Williams. The name was chosen to recognize Williams' hometown of Detroit. The hotel, at Central Avenue and Second Street, complemented the town's depot in architecture. The hotel is still in operation, but additions have been made to each side and the front has been remodeled. (CNB)

BEFORE THE TURN OF THE CENTURY, this was the peaceful scene at First Avenue and Second Street North. Building in foreground at left is the Central Hotel, formerly Rogers House.

JACOB S. DISSTON, Philadelphia industrialist, never lived in St. Petersburg, although his brother, Hamilton Disston, was one of Florida's largest landowners when he purchased four million acres of property at 25 cents an acre. There was a community in St. Petersburg called Disston City (now Gulfport). Jacob Disston invested heavily in various enterprises here and financed F. A. Davis in building his light plant, trolley lines, and other enterprises. He also financed the local telephone company. Disston spent many winters at nearby fashionable Belleair.

St. Petersburg from 1900 to 1920

THIS HANDSOME GENTLEMAN is James Hamilton, the pioneer photographer in St. Petersburg around the turn of the century. Many of his pictures of the era are in the collection of the Pinellas County Historical Commission and included in this volume. (PCHC)

PRETTY FEMALE ATHLETES are these young ladies of St. Petersburg High School about 1900. The photographer, James Hamilton, took this bewitching picture. It is speculated that the letters "P.C.C." on the basketball probably stand for Pinellas County Champions. (PCHC)

Preceding page: ST. PETERSBURG IN 1900, looking northeast from Eighth Avenue and Fourth Street. The Detroit Hotel dominates the downtown skyline, and the waterfront is seen in the distance. (PCHC)

[44]

THE SCHOOL BAND in the early 1900s in front of the first school house. (CNB)

A REAL SHOWPLACE, and conversation piece of the community in 1901, was the Shell Gate Estate, featuring the famous shell fence at the northwest corner of 1st Street North and Second Avenue. The entire archway and garden walls were built of shells gathered from the beaches in the vicinity. Early visitors to this resort city always visited the Shell Fence and mailed post card views of it back home. The fence was built by Owen Albright. (PCHC)

A BEACH VIEW of St. Petersburg about 1900. Those weren't exactly bikinis the ladies were wearing, but they were dressed up for the photograph. (PCHC)

THE LANDING AT PASS-A-GRILLE in 1902: The steamers ran from Tampa to Bradenton and Fort Myers, by way of Pinellas County. The lad with the basket may have been a peanut vendor but at the moment seems to be dreaming of sailing the waters. (PCHC)

"A WONDERFUL COLLECTION OF JUNK" was the description of St. Petersburg's first electric light plant by an early company official. The plant originally served Tarpon Springs but was moved here in 1897. Press accounts of the day boasted "by this enterprise every part of the town is brilliantly illuminated." (PCHC)

THE BRAND NEW First National Bank of St. Petersburg at Second Street South and Central Avenue was opened on February 9, 1903. The St. Petersburg State Bank, the city's first financial institution collapsed in 1902. A new bank, called the West Coast Bank of Florida, was organized with $25,000 capital. It changed its name to First National Bank in 1905. (PCHC)

"WE DESERVE BETTER THAN THIS" was the cry of unhappy St. Petersburg folk when the Atlantic Coast Line Railroad built this new station on the site of the old St. Petersburg Novelty Works between Seventh and Eighth Streets, finishing it on January 27, 1906. The people had complained about the old depot which was a "disgrace to the city," having an inadequate platform, poor lights, and being dirty and too small. The *St. Petersburg Times* editorialized on plans for the new station in its issue of February 11, 1905: "The building will be—just plain wood—with probably a tin roof—which will be a great disappointment to the people of St. Petersburg, and we think ourselves the company should have treated us better as they had always promised to do, but—you know how big corporations are." It had been just a short time before, on December 4, 1906, there had been a citizens indignation meeting protesting the poor service given by ACL. Postmaster Roy S. Hanna produced records which showed that not one of the trains carrying mail had come in on time during the preceding month. He also noted that one train had arrived "only 50 minutes behind schedule—but that had been an unusual occurence. (Boyer)

THE FIRST GARAGE was opened in 1905 by F. W. Ramm & Son. It was on Second Avenue South, between Third and Fourth Streets. The signboard advertised the company as a machine and boiler repair works, and noted that buggies and wagons were repaired, as well as horses shoed. (PCHC)

[48]

LAD CARRIED LARGE PHOTOGRAPH of George Washington on flag to lead the parade in 1907 *(above)*. The boys and girls were dressed in their Sunday clothes for the exciting event. The procession moved to the Opera House where the children performed.

Boys in soldier suits lead the Washington Birthday parade on Central at Fourth in 1908 *(below)*. The original celebration was made possible through the generosity of E. H. Tomlinson who in 1896 presented the local school with 250 silk and bunting American flags and supported the affair in other ways. (Fuller)

GROWN-UPS got into the act, too, when these ladies, dressed as Japanese girls, formed a unit in the Public School Parade on Washington's Birthday, 1907. (CNB)

A "MAY POLE"-type wheel was a feature of the 1910 Washington's Birthday Celebration parade. In 1912, moving pictures were made of the colorful event and shown nation-wide, bringing St. Petersburg some of its first nationwide publicity. (CNB)

"UNCLE SAM" AND "MISS AMERICA" feature the Washinton's Birthday Celebration parade in 1910. And those were real soldiers, probably National Guardsmen, serving as an honor guard for the affair as it moved down Central Avenue. (CNB)

THE FAMOUS "SUNSHINE OFFER" was made by Major Lew B. Brown, then publisher of the *St. Petersburg Independent,* in this full-page ad, published on September 1, 1910. He offered to give away the evening newspaper any day that the sun failed to shine on St. Petersburg. Thus began the image of this city as "The Sunshine City." The newspaper has averaged four days a year of giving away the paper as a result of this unique offer—which still stands. (Dunn)

[51]

THE STEAMER *Manatee* was one of the best known boats which ever plied the waters of Tampa Bay. It was operated by the Independent Line, headed by H. Walter Fuller, which became the Favorite Line. The lines in the area engaged in a "steamship war" over rates. This photo was taken in 1909. (Gandy)

THE STEAMER *H. B. PLANT*, named for the railroad magnate who brought the railroad to Tampa, also was a popular vessel in the heyday of steamships. (Gandy)

[52]

FIRST PRIZE WINNER in the 1913 Festival of States Parade was this beautifully decorated automobile, which has been indentified simply as the "Williams Car." Could it be that the Tournament of Roses in Los Angeles got its know-how from these early day St. Petersburg demonstrators? (Green)

THE FIRST PARADE OF THE FESTIVAL OF STATES was in 1913 and it featured an invasion of the city by gaily-decorated automobiles, shown here on Central Avenue. St. Petersburg residents were to come to like the freedom of movement offered by the automobile, as opposed to mass transportation (Fuller)

[53]

THE POINSETTIA HOTEL was one of the first modern hostelries of St. Petersburg which opened on Saturday evening, December 23, 1911. The proprietors were Dr. G. W. Williamson, Arthur L. Schultz, and Mrs. E. M. Vroom. (Boyer)

ANOTHER FINE HOTEL in the early days of St. Petersburg was the West Coast Inn, featuring large verandahs along its four stories. (Green)

PINELLAS AREA FIGHTS to "secede" from Hillsborough. For years, residents of the Pinellas peninsula, isolated from the county seat at Tampa, had complained of the treatment they received from Hillsborough County officials. Leader in the hot fight to "secede" and begin a new county was civic leader and editor W. L. Straub of the *St. Petersburg Times*. In addition to his withering campaign of criticism of Tampa in the battle to divide the county in his editorials, Editor Straub also socked the Tampa politicians with stinging cartoons. Finally, the 1911 Legislature called a referendum on the division and the voters favored secession by a wide majority. The divorce decree became final on January 1, 1912 when Pinellas County was carved from Hillsborough and became the state's 48th unit. (Dunn)

[55]

NO SOONER had the battle to divide been won than another controversy arose over the site of the county seat for the new Pinellas County. The fight was between St. Petersburg and Clearwater. The latter won by rushing to completion virtually overnight a building to house county government. Here are the first officials of Pinellas County, posing solemnly in front of the new Pinellas County Court House in 1912. They were the School Board: W. A. Allen, Clearwater; A. F. Bartlett, St. Petersburg; A. P. Beckett, Tarpon Springs, and Dixie M. Hollins, County superintendent; C. W. Weicking, St. Petersburg, Clerk of court; Marvel M. Whitehurst, Clearwater, Sheriff; LeRoy Brandon, county judge; J. T. Northrup, Tax Assessor; E. B. (Uncle Eli) McMullen, Tax Collector; A. C. Turner, Treasurer; Albert S. Meares, Supervisor of Registration; and W. S. Rousseau, Surveyor. (CNB)

AVIATION CAME EARLY TO ST. PETERSBURG, and as early as 1912 there was action on the water-front where the airboats zoomed around. There was a hangar there, and thrill-seeking fliers spent all

their spare time talking shop or flying. One of the early dare-devils was Leonard Bonney who put on an exhibition taking off from a Bayboro sandspit on February 19, 1912. (CNB)

[57]

THE FIRST HOME OF the *St. Petersburg Times* was this building at First Avenue South and Third Street. Photo was taken around 1912. The newspaper, descended from the *West Hillsborough Times,* originally published in Clearwater and moved to St. Petersburg in 1892. It became a semi-weekly in 1907, and on January 12, 1912, the first daily edition of *The Times* appeared. (PCHC)

CENTRAL AVENUE, ran from Fourth Street, was a busy thoroughfare by 1912. It appears St. Petersburg had a little pollution problem in those days with smoke stacks belching smoke in the downtown area. Automobiles were fast replacing the horse and buggy. (Boyer)

[58]

WORLD'S FIRST COMMERCIAL AIRLINER was flown by St. Petersburg pilot Tony Jannus, who inaugurated passenger and express service between his home town and Tampa across the bay, on January 1, 1914. News photographers on hand for the inaugural caught this view of Jannus zooming from the St. Petersburg waterfront in his Benoist flying boat. In just 23 minutes, he set the machine down on the Hillsborough River near the present Platt Street bridge. He had scooted along at 50 feet altitude, but *The Tampa Times* reported he could fly as high as 500 feet if he wanted. First paying passenger on the airliner was former St. Petersburg Mayor A. C. Pheil, who paid $400 at auction for the privilege. The flying boat had a 60 horsepower engine and was "chain driven." (Green)

HANDSOME TONY JANNUS is shown here in his flying togs in the cockpit of his airboat. With him is the late Robert F. Russell, an early aviation enthusiast who was an R.A.F. pilot in World War I and was shot down behind the German lines on October 28, 1918. Jannus also was killed during the first World War in 1916 during a test flight in Russia, where he went for the Benoist company. (Anna Russell)

TONY JANNUS with a prominent Floridian in his flying machine, George S. (Dad) Gandy, who was to finish building the famed Gandy Bridge between St. Petersburg and Tampa a decade after this photo was taken in 1914. Jannus, formerly of St. Louis, had set a world's record by flying 2,000 miles from Omaha to New Orleans in continuous, but not sustained, flight. He accomplished this feat just before coming to Florida. The St. Petersburg-Tampa Airboat Line functioned for three months and during that time passengers included such celebrities as Will Rogers and George Ade, top humorists of the day, and Morton Plant, local developer and son of Henry B. Plant who brought the first railroad to the West Coast. (Gandy)

A FLURRY OF REAL ESTATE ACTIVITY started in 1914, but development had not gotten very far at this point on Park Avenue North in the Pasadena section *(above)*. On Central Avenue about 28th Street, looking east, a road building crew is at work *(below)*. (Fuller)

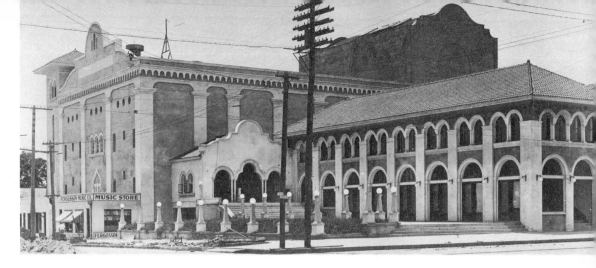

THEY CALLED IT "GANDY'S WHITE ELEPHANT" but his business complex at Central and Fifth featuring the Plaza Theatre proved to be a great success. It was built by George S. Gandy, and opened on March 8, 1913 with Cammaranos' "Il Trovatore" played by the Royal Italian Company. This picture was made in 1914. (Fuller)

THE FIRST CONCRETE BLOCK HOUSE in the city was this structure in Pasadena built in 1916. Walter P. Fuller, a developer and later historian for St. Petersburg, rented the house. (Fuller)

NOW THE MASONIC ORPHANAGE at the north end of Coffee Pot Bayou, this sturdy building originally was a girls' seminary when it was built in 1916 (and this photograph taken). Later, it became the Southland Hotel, operated by the H. Walter Fuller enterprises. (Fuller) [61]

THE SUNSET HOTEL in Sunset Park was way out in the boondocks in 1915—but the 60-room hostelry was a success. The development was at the west end of Central Avenue. The old hotel now is a high-priced retirement home. (Fuller)

DAVISTA, LATER PASADENA, was a development prior to World War I. The brick paving on Second Avenue North came to an abrupt halt at the point photographed here in 1916. But about this time, the City engaged in a big paving project to serve the new subdivision. (Fuller)

DOWNTOWN ST. PETERSBURG in 1916, at Third and Central, looking west. That's the St. Petersburg Hardware Company on the corner at the left. The license plate on the car in the foreground at right was from Pennsylvania and dated 1914. While automobiles and street cars were the chief transportation, also in evidence were bicycles and a dray. (Fuller)

[63]

ST. PETERSBURG FINALLY GOT ITS LIBRARY in 1915, after a campaign for such a building dating back to 1908. Leading the drive to get Carnegie funds was W. L. Straub, editor of the *St. Petersburg Times*. The City provided a site overlooking Mirror Lake. The cornerstone was laid on December 19, 1914, with Governer Park Trammell on hand as principal speaker. The library opened on December 1, 1915, with 2,600 volumes available to the public. The building is still being used; it is now a branch of the main library. (Burgert)

THE GOOD SHIP *H. B. Plant* of the Favorite Line Steamship Company, served the West Coast well. It ran excursions between Tampa and Pass-a-Grille, while its regular weekday run was Tampa. St. Petersburg, Manatee, Bradenton, and return. (Boyer)

[64]

PATRIOTIC ST. PETERSBURG CITIZENS fully supported the war bond drive during World War I. A replica of the Statue of Liberty was erected, along with a "thermometer" showing the city's purchase of the bonds, at Fourth and Central in 1917. The building at that time housed Noel A. Mitchell's office. It later became Walgreen Drug Store, and presently is a woman's clothing store. (Fuller)

CENTRAL NATIONAL BANK at the southwest corner of Fourth and Central in 1917. The canopy behind the Ford car was over the Western Union office. The Ladies Emporium next door was having a "Remodeling Sale". This building was opened in April, 1912, and another floor was added in 1922. (Fuller)

THE NEW ST. PETERSBURG YACHT CLUB building was dedicated on June 15, 1917 *(above)*.
Frank C. Carley was Commodore at the time of this happy occasion and presented the club with a silver
"Commodore's Cup" on which were to appear the club's commodores. Walter P. Fuller is the only
surviving charter member of the club. Below: The yacht club (in foreground) and the yacht basin shortly
after the new building was dedicated. The City Pier is at the left with The Spa on the far side. (Gandy-CNB)

St. Petersburg from 1920 to 1929

THE ST. PETERSBURG TIMES, like Topsy, just "grew and grew." This building went up in 1920 and took care of the needs of the times. It was torn down when the present eight-story Times building was erected in the same location. (Fuller)

SCHOOL OFFICIALS WERE CRITICIZED for erecting a building "too large" for the St. Petersburg High School when this structure went up on Mirror Lake in 1919. But in less than seven years, another and larger high school building had to be constructed. The building in the photo was dedicated February 10, 1920. For many years, the County School Superintendent's office was housed here. The structure later was used for Riviera Junior High. (Fuller)

Preceding page: FIFTH STREET SOUTH in 1921, looking toward Central. At right is the C. M. Roser Building, housing real estate offices of C. M. Roser, one of the early developers of the city including the Roser Park Development. Next to it was Bostain's Cafeteria, then the *St. Petersburg Times* building, brand new at the time. The green benches were popular in those days. (Burgert)

THE FAMOUS "MOTORCYCLE EXTRA" of the *St. Petersburg Times* brought anxious readers news about the disastrous hurricane of 1921. Because the *Times* was without power, an ingenious pressman rigged up a belt to a motorcycle to operate the linotype machine—and kept intact the paper's continuous publication since its founding in 1884. (Dunn)

SECOND St. Petersburg Times EXTRA

St. Petersburg, Fla., Wednesday Morning, Oct. 26, 1921

NO LIVES LOST AT PASS-A-GRILLE
Property Damage May Reach $3,000,000; Two Men Die
TROPICAL STORM SWEEPS CITY

At 1 o'clock today C. E. Letzring, of the Wilhelm Company, returned from Gulport and reported that Captain Sweet had weathered the hurricane at Pass-a-Grille and had brought the news that there had been no loss of life on the island. He said the property loss was heavy.

The sub-chaser 69 left at 10:30 for Pass-a-Grille, carrying Red Cross supplies and a Times representative, but had not returned at 1 o'clock. Wild reports were circulated by other publications that 90 persons had perished. Early estimate of losses in the city and vicinity was lowered to not more than three million.

JAPANESE ARCHITECTURE was popular in 1920—above is the Coffee Pot Golf Club House which had a beautiful Japanese garden; at right, a home built in the early 1920s. It is a frame structure, made of cypress, and believed to be the last house of its style left in St. Petersburg. (CNB)

THIS WAS Gandy Boulevard on November 1, 1922, at 4th Street North about 38th Avenue! The boulevard was to lead to the Gandy Bridge then under construction. This bridge was a dream come true for George S. (Dad) Gandy, a Philadelphian who arrived in 1903, and was instrumental in building the city. "Dad" (with hat) is talking *(center left)* about the bridge with C. C. Carr, an owner of the *St. Petersburg Times,* and an attractive, but unidentified, *Times* feature writer. Watching the progress of construction was a popular pastime, and sightseers could go with boats of the "Gandy Bridge Line" *(bottom left),* or they could use a sporty car called a Ford Roadster *(below)* to drive out to the construction site. (Gandy—Fuller—Gandy)

[70]

THE TOLL GATES were being built in 1923 to collect from motorists entering Gandy Bridge. The bridge opened the following year and became toll-free in 1944, during World War II, when the Federal Government seized the span and lifted the fees, paying Gandy the court-determined value. (Gandy)

AN INTER-URBAN STREET RAILWAY between St. Petersburg and Tampa was contemplated when Gandy Bridge was built, but it never was used even though the rails were included in the structure. Here some dignitaries look at the concrete construction where the space is left for the rails. Early model cars sport AAA emblems. (Gandy)

"Longest Highway Bridge in the World" was the boast when Gandy Bridge was opened in 1924. It was a big step toward opening development of the Pinellas Peninsula. (Roscoe Frey)

THERE WAS A BIG HAPPENING, maybe a Fourth of July celebration, out at Pass-a-Grille Beach Casino the day this picture was taken in 1922. The community was invaded by Tin Lizzies *(above)* bringing picnickers to the beach. "Come and get it!" probably was the cry a few moments later when food and drink were freely dispensed *(below)*. (Gandy)

Preceding page: "PLAY BALL!" was the good news shouted at the height of the spring baseball training season in 1922 when the Boston Braves went into action on the old St. Petersburg Athletic Park, one block north of the site of the present Al Lang Field on the waterfront at St. Petersburg. (CNB)

PASS-A-GRILLE BEACH in the early 1920s had its idyllic spots, as this tranquil scene *(left)* proves. But whether in bathing "costume" or not, you could enjoy the cooling breezes, the shimmering sand, or splash in the surf *(below).* (Burgert)

THE OLD CASINO on Pass-a-Grille Beach was the locale for much merry-making until it burned down. (Burgert)

THE THEATRE that was built backward is how they described the Pheil Theatre on Central Avenue near Fourth Street, finally completed in 1924 as a hotel and movie house. The movie fans entered the theatre under the screen and walked toward the back of the theatre to find their seats. A. C. Pheil, former Mayor of St. Petersburg, owner of the building, designed it that way so he could add several store spaces to the theatre. With the screen on the south end of the building, it was possible to provide store space on the street. The arrangement also made it easier to empty the theatre in case of fire. The Pheil Theatre was one of the first theatres in the country to have "talkies" and the second in Florida to boast this innovation. (Gandy)

FIRST MODERN FIRE-RESISTANT SCHOOL in the city in the mid-1920s was St. Petersburg Senior High School at the present site of the County building on Fifth Street North between First and Second Avenues. (Fuller)

ORIGINALLY THE MASON HOTEL (which opened in 1924), the landmark at right is now the Princess Martha Hotel on the northwest corner of Fourth Street and First Avenue North. The Mason hotel went bankrupt and was acquired by William Muir who renamed it to honor his wife Martha. (Burgert)

FIRST UNITED METHODIST CHURCH it is called now, but originally it was the First Methodist Church. The present building was erected in 1925 at Third Street and Second Avenue North. The church was organized in 1889, and its first building rose in 1892. The present building is one of downtown St. Petersburg's most attractive landmarks. (Burgert)

[77]

ST. PETERSBURG HIGH SCHOOL overlooking a tranquil lake. This Senior High School was moved in 1925 to 5th Avenue North and 26th Street. This building became, then, the home of St. Petersburg Junior High School. (Burgert)

THE BRAND NEW SORENO HOTEL, a million-dollar hostelry, opened on January 1, 1924. Before the month had passed, it was filled to capacity. It was built by Soren Lund who immigrated from his native Denmark at age 14—with only $13 to his name, and no friends or relatives to assist him. (Burgert)

JOHNNY GREEN'S FLYING MA-CHINE, a hydroplane named "Betty," was the talk of the town in 1923. Green had succeeded Tony Jannus as the city's early bird. Green and Albert Whitted, another aviation pioneer, had adjoining hangars on Spa Beach, but, according to historian Ralph Reed, they did not speak to each other. (Fuller)

STRAUB PARK on St. Petersburg's waterfront gave this appearance in December 1924. The attractive park was named in honor of W. L. Straub, editor of the *St. Petersburg Times,* who had fought in the early years for preservation of the waterfront for public purposes. The Spa beach and pier is seen off to the left. (Burgert)

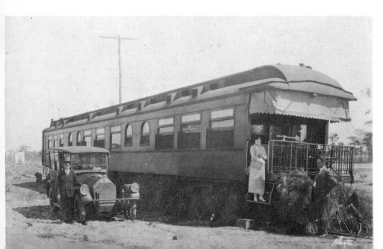

MOST FLAMBOYANT PROMOTER in St. Petersburg during the real estate boom was Jack Taylor, who cut a wide swath in the business and social circles of the bustling city. Here he's seen in 1924 with his wealthy wife Evelyn at their private railroad car, along with their chauffeur and Pierce Arrow limousine (Fuller)

THE MAGNIFICENT ROLYAT HOTEL built by Jack Taylor has been a landmark through the years. It was later used by the Florida Military academy before becoming the Stetson University College of Law. The name "Rolyat," by the way, is "Taylor" spelled backwards. (Burgert)

[80]   ANOTHER VIEW OF THE ROLYAT HOTEL in Gulfport as it looked during the boom. (Burgert)

THE ORNATE LOBBY OF The Rolyat Hotel was an attraction during the Florida boom. Jack Taylor, the builder, came to St. Petersburg in 1921 right after the devastating hurricane of that year, but was impressed with the potential of St. Petersburg, and set about to develop Pasadena and other sections of the boom-time city. Walls of the Rolyat lobby were pink, the columns, sand color (dull salmon), the beams dark brown, and the ceiling decorations, white, blue, and red. (Fuller)

PRETTY GIRLS decorate the wishing well on the patio of the Rolyat Hotel. The publicity photo was made during the boom. (Green)

THE PLUS-FOUR KNICKERBOCKER was the popular "uniform" of real estate salesmen during the Florida boom. Some are seen here in the patio of the Rolyat Hotel. The dapper promoter, Jack Taylor, is seen in the center of the group in white "ice cream" trousers. Among those in the photograph are Innes Henry, George Cummins, and Roy Cummins. (Fuller)

THE UNIQUE OPEN-AIR POST OFFICE on Fourth Street has been a landmark since it was first built in 1917. This view, taken in 1925, shows the Princess Martha Hotel at right, the Suwannee Hotel in the background at left: Snell & Hamlett's real estate business in the left foreground was busily selling North shore property. The Post Office was considered unique at the time, because patrons could reach their boxes even when the Post Office was closed—which was a novelty at the time. (Burgert)

ST. PETERSBURG'S FINEST in 1925. The Police Chief, during this period, was James Coslick (1923-1928). Coslick was appointed in 1923 to succeed Chief Edward J. Bidaman, who was fired by the City Commission during a power struggle. For a short time both chiefs claimed to be the top officer; but in March 1924 a court decided that Coslick was the legal chief. (CNB)

[82]

THE FLORIDA THEATRE was built in 1925, and entertained the community for years. William Powell and Myrna Loy were starring in "After the Thin Man" the day this photograph was taken. In the late 1960s the First National Bank bought and demolished it, and the rest of the eight-story building at the northeast corner of First Avenue South and Fifth Street. (Green)

THE FIRST BAPTIST CHURCH in downtown St. Petersburg, next door to the Princess Martha Hotel, is a handsome building. This structure was erected in 1923, and this photo was taken a few years later. The church was first organized in St. Petersburg in 1892. (Burgert)

THE GREAT COLISEUM at Fourth Avenue North and Fifth Street has been the capital of entertainment for St. Petersburg fun-lovers since its fabulous opening in November 1924. The mammoth structure, known affectionately as the "barn," cost $250,000 to build and has hosted countless social events, conventions, exhibits, and sports competitions. (Burgert)

FLORIDA'S FIRST SHOPPING CENTER was Jungle Prado built in 1925 by Walter P. Fuller. Its shops were most popular, and even lady guests from the fashionable Belleview Biltmore Hotel at Belleaire came here to browse and buy. The well-known Gangplank Restaurant was also located in Jungle Prado. (Burgert)

BEAUTIFUL RESIDENTIAL AREAS. such as this one in North St. Petersburg about 1925, have always made the city an attrative place in which to live. (Burgert)

LIKE ANTS AT A PICNIC, people and their automobiles packed the beaches at St. Petersburg on June 17, 1926, to cool off. (Burgert)

THE ALTA MARINA project was started in 1925 by James Stephenson Sr., between 56th and 62nd Avenues South, from Fourth Street East to Tampa Bay. According to Walter Fuller, the project was a failure on its first try, despite the fact the land area was good. The second try, in 1929 by Robert Lyons of Washington, also failed. This photo was taken in 1926. (Burgert)

THE MILLION DOLLAR PIER and yacht basin in foreground were busy places on March 23, 1926. The lovely Soreno Hotel dominates the skyline on the mainland. (Burgert)

THE PLAZA THEATRE is seen in the foreground, at right, in this scene at Central Avenue and Fifth Street in 1926. The "main drag" was not as congested in those days as it is nowadays. (Burgert)

Following page: A BOOM TIME VIEW of St. Petersburg, taken in 1925, and looking at Mirror Lake, with the Suwannee Hotel in the center. (Fuller)

THE SWANK VINOY PARK HOTEL, facing Tampa Bay on partly filled ground at Fifth Avenue North, was one of the 10 fine new hotels built in St. Petersburg during the Florida real estate boom. It was the project of the Aymer Vinoy Laughner, whose family had made it big in oil in Pennsylvania. Like other structures of the day, this was of Mediterranean architecture. (Burgert)

THE POPULAR PRINCESS MARTHA HOTEL in downtown St. Petersburg formerly was the Mason Hotel. It was a beehive of activity on January 18, 1926, and continues to be popular half a century later. In recent years guests have included Mrs. Muriel Humphrey, wife of Senator Hubert Humphrey, and entertainers Liberace, Danny Thomas, and Van Cliburn. (Burgert)

THE SPECTACULAR FESTIVAL OF STATES PARADE featured floats as elaborate in 1926 as today. Thousands of sun-drenched Winter visitors line Central Avenue to admire the beautiful units. Flag-decorated building at left is the old American Bank and Trust Co., built in 1913. This firm is unrelated to today's firm of the same name. The old building at 340 Central Avenue, featuring handsome columns and metal paneling, is now occupied by the Thomson & McKinnon Auchincloss Inc. stock brokerage. (Burgert)

Facing page: PASADENA was one of St. Petersburg's most beautiful golf courses during the boom years. It was opened in 1926 with a sensational exhibition match between golfing greats, Walter Hagen and Bobby Jones. (Burgert)

THE GREAT WALTER HAGEN, one of the most famous of golf pros, was the pro at Pasadena Golf Course in 1925. He's shown here standing on step of car. Note the fancy golf bag the golfer is transporting on the running board of his vehicle. (Fuller)

GOLFING CAME INTO ITS OWN in St. Petersburg during the Florida real estate boom. And the big names in the game helped put it over. Here are the great Bobby Jones and Walter Hagen performing at the Pasadena course in 1925. Jones is doing the putting. (Fuller)

[92]

THE JUNGLE COUNTRY CLUB was another well-played course. The original club was known as the St. Petersburg Country Club, built and opened in 1915. But in 1924, during the boom, the Allen-Fuller Company purchased the property and renamed it the Jungle Club. Walter P. Fuller says that the Jungle Golf Course was the city's first good standard golf course. (Burgert)

A DOWNTOWN BEACH is Spa Beach in the North Yacht Basin. It's been a popular spot for years, whether for the "Sunrise Club" *(above)*, doing morning exercises, or for sunbathers and swimmers *(below)*. (CNB—Burgert)

WHAT A VIEW of St. Petersburg's waterfront! It shows the Goodyear blimp which spent many winters here, but now stays in Miami. Here the blimp floats gently over the famous Million Dollar Pier, yacht basin, and Spa beach *(above)*. The pier was built in 1926 and offered this Mediterranean-style casino *(facing page)* as headquarters for fun during the season. This particular pier was razed later to make way for a new one which was finished in the early 1970s. (Burgert—CNB)

FOR 32 YEARS, C. PERRY SNELL had masterminded a number of highly successful subdivisions, with glamourous names such as Bayshore, Bay Front, Bay View, North Shore, and Granada Terrace. Then came the climax, development of the exclusive Snell Isle in the mid-1920s. This montage shows some of the features that made Snell Isle stand out. Top left is Snell's beautiful home which featured a third-floor gallery of miniature pictures (third row, right). In third row left is the fancy Snell Isle Golf Club House, while in the bottom row right is an apartment house. Snell is shown in the center oval. In lower row left is the entrance of Snell Isle Park. A rose garden on Snell Isle is seen, top row right. (Fuller)

[98]

RESIDENCE

AN OVERHEAD VIEW of the Snell residence on Snell Isle. Snell was a native of Kentucky, educated as a pharmacist, and was a druggist for 17 years. He first came to St. Petersburg on his honeymoon in 1899. He invested in property while on the trip, but did not come to St. Petersburg to stay until 1904. (Green)

A LILY POOL in the Snell Isle complex. (Green)

A CELEBRITY who built *(below)* on Snell Isle was Billy DeBeck, famed cartoonist who created the comic "Spark Plug and Barney Google." Like other residences *(above)* in the development, DeBeck's attractive home was of Mediterranean design. (Fuller—Green)

TOP FLIGHT ENTERTAINMENT was in store for members of the Snell Isle Golf Club who crowded the dance terrace for social events. (Green)

Snell-Arcade
St. Petersburg. Fla. 1929

THE OFFICE OF SNELL ISLE INC. was the striking Snell Arcade building downtown at Fourth Street North and Central Avenue, now the Rutland Building *(preceding page)*. Exquisite tile, Italian mosaics, and statuary dressed up Snell Arcade to attract the public to its fancy shops. Among the figures were Thorwaldsen's Hebe, Gaby's Diana, Canova's Venus, Venus Danzatrice, Venus de Medici, Venus de Milo, Venus Falconnet, etc. (Fuller—Green)

LIVELY SPANISH DANCERS used to perform on the roof garden atop Snell Arcade. (Green)

ANOTHER C. PERRY SNELL project was the boom-time development of the North shore section called Granada Terrace. It was a highly restricted, exclusive section for Spanish and Italian stucco homes. Not only the type of house, but also the exterior, the color scheme, and the landscaping of the grounds were controlled in the restrictions. (Burgert)

THE ST. PETERSBURG CHESS-CHECKER-DOMINO CLUB in Waterfront Park was a busy place during the 1920s. Some of the overflow from the inside enjoy checkers—and the famed sunshine—at the same time. Note the handsome sailor straws and the caps, popular head dress of the day. (Burgert)

Preceding page: LOOKING ACROSS MIRROR LAKE toward downtown St. Petersburg in 1926. (Burgert)

[106]

HORSESHOE-PLAYING CAPITAL of the world was St. Petersburg during the zany days of the Florida real estate boom. The sign on the press box at the Mirror Lake center shows this was competition among Ohio visitors here. The exciting matches thrilled both participants and spectators. The players were real pros. Note shade was provided by pine straw over net. (Burgert)

LEGENDARY PUBLICIST, JOHN LODWICK, developed the World Horseshoe Championships here and they were held in 1919, 1921, 1922, 1926, 1927, 1928, and 1929. Photo taken at the Sunshine Pleasure Club on February 14, 1927, shows competitors in the tourney that year. The tourneys attracted the press of the nation, albeit the stories they sent back home were sometimes tongue-in-cheek pieces. Robert Maxwell, a reporter for the *Philadelphia Public Ledger* described the 1922 event like this: "Long gray clusters of Spanish moss hung from the branches and this blended with the frosted hirsute adornment which hung limply from the chins of a majority of the gentlemen in the audience. Charles Clyde Davis, Columbus, Ohio carpenter, is the new king of the steel oxfords. He slammed Ralph Spencer for a row of palmetto bushes, 50 to 29 points . . . they were hurling ringers with reckless abandon. The equestrian footwear was closely examined to see that no loaded shoes were rung in. This would have been very hard on the wrists." (CNB)

SHUFFLEBOARD WAS INTRODUCED to the U.S. in Florida. It started in 1913 at Daytona Beach and soon spread across the country. Every community had its own rules, so in 1924 a conference was called at St. Petersburg of all state shuffleboard clubs by City Recreation Director Pierce V. Gahan. And there the modern form of shuffleboard was defined. It's a game for the whole family, but it is especially popular with older citizens. Shuffleboard was played in England in the fifteenth century, and was originally called shovelboard. It is said that Henry VIII issued a royal decree forbidding its play because it prevented the proper practice of archery. The decree didn't stop these modern St. Petersburg shufflers! (Burgert)

SOMETHING TO ENTERTAIN EVERY-
ONE has long been the objective of St.
Petersburg for its winter visitors. The
gentlemen *above* were having a big time
playing roque at Mirror Lake in the boom
days, while the well-dressed ladies at right
indulged in a game of lawn bowling.
(Burgert—Fuller)

SAILING IS A TRADEMARK of down-
town St. Petersburg in the 1920s. The vessels
are in front of the Yacht Club with the
Soreno Hotel in the background. (Burgert)

ST. PETERSBURG BEACH in its natural state in the 1920s—a tranquil scene in easy driving distance from the city. An early vintage car is shown nosing around the bend in the sand road. (Green)

[110]

MIRROR LAKE is an oasis in downtown St. Petersburg and a superb spot to enjoy Florida living. (Burgert)

THE UBIQUITOUS GREEN BENCHES of St. Petersburg have provided rest spots for shoppers and visitors since former Mayor Noah Mitchell introduced them in 1907. They were proclaimed to be painted green by Mayor Al Lang in 1914, but in recent years the City decided they should be in pastel colors. (Burgert)

THE PATIO THEATRE was on the north side of Central Avenue between First and Second Avenue North. (Burgert)

CENTRAL AVENUE. The pretty tower-topped building in far center is the Snell Arcade, now the Rutland Building. Beyond it is the old West Coast Title Company building, now the First Federal Savings & Loan Association of St. Petersburg, at Fourth Street. (Green)

THE HAAS MUSEUM is housed in the homelike atmosphere of this two-story home and in the Grace Turner House next to it. Other exhibits are contained in buildings in back of the property and in a train depot and caboose located in a side yard. The huge banyan tree on the left is more than 75 years old. In the front of the house may be seen a hitching post and a watering trough. (CNB)

ANTIQUE KITCHEN ACCESSORIES *(below left)* in the Grace Turner House representing an era long before electric labor-saving gadgets became available to modern housewives. Another exhibit is the Child's Bedroom *(below right)*. Note the fancy potty under the bed. (CNB)

[113]

A FINE HOTEL NAMED FOR AN OPERA STAR is the elegant Don Ce-sar on St. Petersburg Beach *(center)*. It was begun in 1925 by Thomas J. Rowe, a shrewd, courtly, and frail New Englander who came to St. Petersburg during the Florida Boom and escalated a $21,000 bankroll into a fortune of over a million dollars. Even though the real estate boom was about over, Rowe continued to erect the pink stucco castle, against the advice of his real estate advisor, Walter P. Fuller *(left, without jacket)*. Finally, on Jan. 16, 1928 the doors of the posh hostelry opened. "I told Rowe it would break him and kill him and it did," Fuller said. "But he had no regrets." Rowe died in 1940. He had named the hotel for his favorite opera star, Don Caesar de Bazan in the opera, "Maritana." Don Ce-Sar Hotel guests had their own fine Gulf beach to play on *(bottom)*. (Fuller—Burgert)

St. Petersburg since 1930

A SPECIAL EVENT DREW A LARGE CROWD to Albert Whitted Airport along St. Petersburg's waterfront in 1933. (CNB)

Preceding page: COLLAPSE of the Florida real estate boom and the stock market crash set the stage for a bank and economic crisis in St. Petersburg as the new decade of the Thirties go underway. Several local banks failed in 1930. Others dropped by the wayside. The last of the old group of banks to survive was the Central National Bank at Central Avenue and Fourth Street the southwest corner. It had weathered two runs, according to Walter P. Fuller, and finally succumbed in the Summer of 1931. This dramatic photo shows the panic run on Central National on that fateful day. Fuller reports that upon liquidation, Central National paid off the greatest percentage of any of the banks to its depositors—53 percent. The First National did almost as well, paying back 42 percent. (Green)

ONE OF THE FIRST 250 FLIERS of the United States Navy was J. Albert Whitted *(right)*, his pilot's number being 179. He attended public schools in St. Petersburg and established a cycle shop, offering the Indian motorcycle. He enlisted in the Navy on March 17, 1917, earned his lieutenant's commission on September 25, 1918, and served as chief instructor of advanced flying at the Pensacola Naval Air Station. He was in full charge of air manoeuvers at Guantanamo Bay, Cuba, in February 1919. After the war, Whitted did commercial flying from his home town. On August 19, 1923, Albert Whitted and four passengers were killed when his Falcon plane broke a propellor in flight near Pensacola. The Albert Whitted Airport *(below)* honors the name of this local hero. (Fuller)

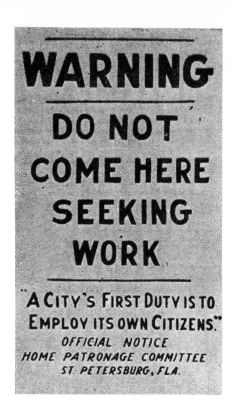

A GOOD PLACE TO VISIT—but don't come to stay was the idea of this sign erected at the city limits of St. Petersburg during the depth of the depression. Jobs were hard to come by, and placards were set up at the entrances to town to discourage transients. This was the era when men without jobs worked on weed gangs for $1 a day, where hard-hit landowners marched on City Hall to protest taxes, the townspeople survived on WPA jobs, and City officials called on Washington for more funds for relief projects.

HAPPY DAYS ARE HERE AGAIN was a tune making the rounds during the early 1930's, depression or no depression, and these bathing beauties seem to bear out the words of the song. (CNB)

SWIMMING was a favorite activity for residents and visitors alike. This closeup shot *(left)* reveals what the well-dressed swimmer wore in 1931 in St. Petersburg. (CNB–Green)

BUSY CENTRAL AVENUE at Fifth Street looking East, as it appeared in the early 1930's. The Pheil Hotel in the background was built in 1924 by former Mayor A. C. Pheil. Its name in recent years was the Madison Hotel; it was shut down as a hotel in 1973. (Burgert)

THE EVOLUTION OF THE BICYCLE is demonstrated by some publicity dolls in St. Petersburg. Miss Dora Chenneville of Dayton, Ohio, a visitor, is riding the highboy, while Patricia Woolson of Wildwood, N.J., is guiding the 100-year-old pusher. Identity of the third lass on the modern wheels is lost. (CNB)

PUBLICITY PHOTOS have been the life-blood of St. Petersburg's tourism through the years. Here's one which hit the wire services in the early 1930's. It shows "Freckles" Ackerman and his freckled friend and carries that all-important dateline "St. Petersburg, Fla." The city has had many great publicity chiefs, including John Lodwick and Pressly C. Phillips. It was Lodwick who set up such national eye-catchers as the "Purity League." He talked an obliging lady into fussing about the length of bathing suits worn at Spa Beach. The natural follow-up, then, was for St. Petersburg's handsome mayor, Frank Fortune Pulver, dolled up in his spotless white suit, and a policeman to visit the beach and solemnly measure suits on display to the public eye. All this, while Lodwick recorded the "raid" for the press. (CNB)

[122]

FABULOUS FLOATS make the Festival of States Parade of 1930 one of the prettiest in the country. Here's the New York state entry; the Massachusetts float recalls the Boston Tea Party; and a giant cash register asserts that "Ohio Registers the Money of the World." (CNB)

[123]

FENCING was a popular sport in 1931 and these young ladies were taking lessons on Spa Beach—again while the publicity bureau was busy shooting pictures for the nation's newspapers and magazines. (CNB)

DOG RACING HAS BEEN POPULAR in St. Petersburg for decades. Here is a view of Derby Lane in the early 1930's. (Burgert)

THE FAMOUS KIDS AND KUBS, the Three-Quarter-Century Softball Club at St. Petersburg, plays three games a week at North Shore Park. A candidate for active membership in this distinctive ball club must have passed his 74th birthday anniversary. The club was founded during the winter season of 1930-31. (CNB) [125]

AND THEN THERE's THE PELS AND GULLS. Almost as famous as the Kids and Kubs are the Pels and Gulls, the Half-Century Softball Club in the Sunshine City. It, too, plays three games weekly at North Shore Park. It was founded in the early 1930's—and its players must be 50 years old or over. (CNB)

SUDDENLY IT'S SPRING and Al Lang
Field at St. Petersburg comes to life with
big league baseball spring training underway *(below)*. Shirt-sleeved spectators, here
for the winter, train their cheering lungs as
they watch the exhibitions. The great
Bambino *(right)* and St. Petersburg had a
love affair while he was at the height of his
baseball career. George Herman Ruth—
just call him "Babe"—is shown here in
civvies with his boss, Marse Joe McCarthy,
manager of the New York Yankees. Babe
hit 60 home runs for the Yankees in 1927,
and his total was 714 homers. He also was
a great pitcher for the Boston Red Sox before he was sold to the Yanks. He was a
showman, too, was "The Sultan of Swat,"
and often would notify the fans in advance
just when and where he was going to blast
it out of the park. (Green)

A LOOK AT St. Petersburg from the air in 1932. Fifth Street is in the center, looking northwest toward Mirror Lake. The *St. Petersburg Times* plant is seen in the center foreground. (Burgert)

NATIONAL AIRLINES SYSTEM

ALBERT WHITTED MUNICIPAL AIRPORT, P. O. BOX 868, ST. PETERSBURG, FLORIDA

·G. T. Baker, General Manager·

RESERVATIONS

Southbound—Wire National Airlines System, 305 West Adams Street, Jacksonville, Florida.

Northbound—Wire National Airlines System, Municipal Airport St. Petersburg, Florida.

HOTELS—TRAVEL BUREAUS—TELEGRAPH OFFICES

Jacksonville-St. Petersburg

1 Daily	Mls.	TABLE 97 Eastern Standard Time	2 Daily
AM 8 00	0	Lv.....JACKSONVILLE.....Ar	PM 6 40
9 00	98	Lv.....DAYTONA BEACH.....Lv	5 50
9 43	149	Lv.....ORLANDO.....Lv	5 10
10 28	208	Lv.....LAKELAND.....Lv	4 25
11 03	244	Lv.....TAMPA.....Lv	3 50
11 15	264	Ar.....ST. PETERSBURG.....Lv	3 35
AM			PM

LIGHT FACE—ONE WAY   DARK FACE—ROUND TRIP

FARES	Daytona Beach	Jacksonville	Lakeland	Orlando	St. Petersburg	Tampa
Daytona Beach	....	5.64 **10.34**	7.29 **13.13**	4.00 **8.00**	10.60 **19.08**	9.59 **17.27**
Jacksonville	5.64 **10.34**	....	12.93 **23.28**	9.37 **16.87**	16.68 **30.03**	15.23 **27.42**
Lakeland	7.29 **13.13**	12.93 **23.28**	....	4.00 **8.00**	4.50 **9.00**	3.00 **6.00**
Orlando	4.00 **8.00**	9.37 **16.87**	4.00 **8.00**	....	6.18 **11.13**	5.80 **9.44**
St. Petersburg	10.60 **19.08**	16.68 **30.03**	4.50 **9.00**	6.18 **11.13**	....	3.00 **6.00**
Tampa	9.59 **17.27**	15.23 **27.42**	3.00 **6.00**	5.80 **9.44**	3.00 **6.00**	....

U. S. MAIL   PASSENGERS   EXPRESS

THE 1935 TIMETABLE *(left)* of National Airlines shows the line headquartered at St. Petersburg's Albert Whitted Airport and with service only between St. Petersburg and Jacksonville. Pretty stewardesses have been a trade mark of National Airlines since its early days. (Dunn—W. E. Foss)

Facing page: AN AIRLINE WAS BORN in St. Petersburg in 1934 with the award to National Airlines of a 142-mile mail route between this city and Daytona Beach, via Tampa, Lakeland, and Orlando. The first flight was on October 15. The "fleet" consisted of two second-hand Ryan aircraft (similar to those shown in the top photo). The airline had five employees, including G. T. (Ted) Baker the dauntless and perservering architect of National Airlines, who is shown here *(center,* in shirtsleeves) proudly displaying National's 10-passenger Stinson in 1936. The plane cruised at 130 m.p.h. The spectacular growth of NAL started just 40 days after the line began operations. Because of airport alterations at Daytona Beach, service was extended to Jacksonville, and by early 1935 business had increased so much that two eight-passenger, trimotor Stinson planes, with a top speed of 125 m.p.h., were needed to handle the traffic. During the winter of 1936-37, a twice weekly service was started by National Airlines between St. Petersburg and Miami. In 1938 service was extended to New Orleans. The company relocated its general offices and principal base of operations to Jacksonville in 1939. With the expansion of services and the rapid increase in traffic, three 17-place Lockheed Lodestars *(bottom),* luxury planes with a top speed of 280 miles an hour, were purchased in November 1940. Bringing the first of these new planes from the factory at Burbank, Calif., "Ted" Baker broke the transcontinental speed record by flying the 2,357 miles from Burbank to Jacksonville in nine hours and 29 minutes which included time on the ground at Dallas for refueling. (NAL)

THIS "MODERN," FOUR-STORY MOUND PARK HOSPITAL was built in 1937 at a cost of $204,825 at Seventh Street and Sixth Avenue South. Nurses are on the steps of the then famous Shell Mound in "Shell Mound Park." This park next to the hospital was purchased by the city in 1909 for $1,500. The shell mound is no longer in existence. The first hospital at this location was the St. Petersburg Emergency Hospital, opened on July 28, 1910. The second was the Augusta Memorial, opened in March, 1913. The name was later changed to City Hospital, and still later, in 1923, the name was again changed to Mound Park. It is now a private institution called Bayfront Medical Center, Inc. (CNB)

A LANDMARK since 1933 has been the attractive Bay Pines Veterans Hospital on Bay Pines Boulevard. The U.S. Government Hospital is located on Boca Ceiga Bay and has a large, pine-shaded, park-like grounds. (CNB)

THE EQUITABLE BUILDING at Fourth Street and Central Avenue is a landmark from the boom days.
The 10-story skyscraper originally belonged to the West Coast Title Co., and it was opened on July 10, 1926.
A news story in *The Evening Independent* proudly proclaimed: "With its chaste, slender lines rising 10
stories above the street level, the West Coast Title building is considered one of the finest examples of
Gothic architecture, as applied to office building construction, in the whole south." West Coast Title was
originally formed by John D. Harris in 1912. In 1938, the Equitable Building was sold to the First Federal
Savings & Loan Association of St. Petersburg. It has since been modernized with a new "skin" and
continues to house the firm. (Fuller)

[131]

THE PARK CAFETERIA building at the southwest corner of Third Street and First Avenue North. (Green)

THOSE FAMED GREEN BENCHES of St. Petersburg are getting a fine workout in this photograph. It's a wonderful way to sit and watch the world go by. (Burgert)

THE WORLD'S MOST UNUSUAL DRUG STORE is what they called Doc Webb's emporium. James Earl Webb *(right)* known mostly as "Doc," came to St. Petersburg on 1925 and, with an associate, opened a tiny drug store on Ninth Street and Second Avenue South. Within weeks, "Doc" bought out his partner, and then initiated the dramatic retail operations that created—and characterized—Webb's City. There are 77 "retail stores" under one roof now, with more than 1,500 employees—and 60,000 customers daily. The original store, started with $5,000 accumulated savings, occupied a rented space only 17 by 28 feet. A native of Tennessee, "Doc" Webb is a town character, the darling of the senior citizen who finds all kinds of bargains at his place that help them to stretch a pension during inflation times. An apt description of this dynamic merchant comes from the pen of Ernie Pyle, the great wartime correspondent, who wrote for the little people, in an interview with "Doc": "He talks 'country' Tennessee talk and is as nervous as a witch. He is flexed, fixed, strained for the leap. He is as sharp as the serpent's tooth . . . Doc Webb was born nervous and keyed up. An uncanny lightning strikes within him a million times a day. All the time he keeps winding up, like an airplane motor in a dive . . . " (Webb–Burgert)

[133]

WEBB'S POSTER GIRLS have appeared from coast to coast and have been featured on television including the Ed Sullivan Show. Webb's Poster Girls such as Janet Crockett *(left),* who became a "Miss Florida" and was runner-up in the Miss America contest, were chosen from thousands of applicants, and Doc's keen eye for beauty picks the winners. Here is one bevy of Poster Girls *(below)* that reaped untold millions in publicity both for Webb's City and St. Petersburg. (Webb)

SERVICE CLUBS in St. Petersburg pool efforts to enter this glamorous float in a Festival of States Parade in the 1930s. (Burgert)

"OUR LANDLORD says get out and stay out!" was the only slogan that Mather Good and Bad Furniture needed to stage a "Everything Must Go" furniture sale in the 1930s. (Green)

THE WILLSON-CHASE STORE on Central Avenue in 1909 through a merger of E. B. Willson with Beulah Chase, and celebrated its 50th anniversary in 1959. It passed from the business scene downtown [137] in 1965. But here's a photo showing much activity in vicinity of the store in earlier days. (Green)

THE LAST HOME of the *St. Petersburg Independent* before the paper was acquired by its rival, the *Times*. (Green)

ACTIVITY at Central Avenue and Fifth Street, featuring the Plaza Theatre and Hotel, the so-called "Gandy's Folly" of pioneer builder, George S. Gandy. (Green)

[138]

AERIAL of Admiral Farragut Academy on Fifth Avenue and Park Street North. In the foreground is an inlet off Boca Ceia Bay. The property originally was the St. Petersburg Country Club, but its plans never developed, and during the boom of the 1920s Walter P. Fuller built this structure as an elegant hotel. The military school subsequently acquired it. (CNB)

THE ST. PETERSBURG-BRADENTON FERRY did a land office business during its existence, before it was put out of business by the construction of the Sunshine Skyway bridge between the two Gulf cities. This photo was taken at the Piney Point Station in 1937. (Burgert)

THE ORIGINAL First National Bank Building at Central and Fifth, the site of which is now occupied by the Florida National Bank. (Fuller)

BEAUTIES, BIRDS, AND CONCERTS: There are a lot of attractions in Williams Park in downtown St. Petersburg. These young lovelies *(above)* enjoyed feeding the pigeons, while record crowds flock to [141] Williams Park to attend the concerts. The shady spot along Fourth Street is still popular with winter visitors and home folks alike. (Burgert–Green)

THE CENTER OF INTEREST in Williams Park is the ultra-modern band shell with a blue glass roof, which shelters the famed Joe Lefter's band, an assembly of musicians from many of the nation's famed old-time bands, such as Sousa's, Pryor's, Conway's, and Krill's. Five thousand or more fans pour into the park for the musical treat. (Green)

THE PINELLAS AIRPORT seemed to be rather active when this photo was taken in its earlier days.
(Burgert)

PASADENA COMMUNITY CHURCH on 70th Street South was started in 1925, but did not "catch fire" until 1929 when the late Rev. J. Wallace Hamilton was assigned. Soon overflow crowds jammed the church and church yards, and loud speakers brought the proceedings to those who could not get inside. As many as 10,000 persons have been on hand for Easter services. (Burgert)

ST. PETERSBURG'S "NATIONAL BIRD" is the pelican. Winter visitors marvel at the fun of feeding and photographing this friendly, giant bird along the municipal pier. (CNB—Burgert)

FOURTH STREET SOUTH, looking north from Third Avenue South. The Tramor Restaurant is in the first business building shown. (Burgert)

THE MUNICIPAL BUILDING or City Hall was erected in 1939 at 175 Fifth Street North. Its total cost including equipment and furnishings was $389,415. The contractor and builder was R. E. "Rube" Clarson. (CNB)

CHAMBER OF COMMERCE building in the early 1940s is seen in this picture. The line is composed of out-of-state tourists from all parts of the United States and Canada registering their home towns. (CNB)

THE SECOND VERSION of the *St. Petersburg Times* building. (Fuller)

CITY HALL and the Chamber of Commerce building. Parking space was at a premium but no parking meters yet in sight. (Green)

[148]

THE VINOY HOTEL, in the background, was head-quarters for the U.S. Army Air Force men who trained in St. Petersburg during World War II. This is one of the publicity photos taken during that time. (CNB)

THE SIGN ON THE BEACH at the Don Ce-Sar Hotel declares the property to be a "Military Reservation" during World War II. The young airman and his girl friend snatch a few moments of relaxation on the clean, beach on the Gulf of Mexico. (Dunn)

SHUFFLEBOARD WAS A FAVORITE SPORT in St. Petersburg in 1943. The sport, here, dates back to 1922 when W. N. Britten of Rochester, N.Y. came to town. He had played shuffleboard on shipboard, liked it, and finally got it adopted here. (CNB)

DONKEY BASEBALL, frustrating for players, but fun for spectators, was a novelty sport that swept the country in the early 1940's. This picture was taken at Waterfront Park in St. Petersburg at the height of the craze. (CNB)

BEACHFRONT COTTAGES were damaged by a storm that swept through Sunset Beach, south of Treasure Island (now called St. Petersburg Beach), on June 26, 1945. There have been more serious disasters than this in the past. Bathers are seen in the water, so the danger must have passed when this photo was made. (Burgert)

[151]

[152] POST-WAR DEVELOPMENT enabled National Airlines to modernize its fleet with these sporty DC-6s, delivered in December 1946. These planes carried 58 to 60 passengers at 300 miles an hour. On June 1, 1946 National moved its general offices to Miami from Jacksonville, and continues to operate from that city. This photo shows the DC-6 zooming over Miami Beach skyline. (NAL)

AL LANG FIELD in 1947. This is where the action is during the spring baseball training each year. It's named for former St. Petersburg Mayor Al Lang who was instrumental in bringing the big leaguers to Florida in 1914. (Burgert)

THE *HMS* Bounty, famed ship used the Metro-Goldwyn-Mayer movie, is now on permanent exhibit at St. Petersburg. To keep the exact replica of the original eighteenth century vessel ship-shape, master craftsman Clarence Carlson is constantly busy doing repair work. (Dunn)

Preceding page: THE *Joseph Conrad* was a maritime training ship when she was stationed at Bayboro Harbor in St. Petersburg during the war. (CNB)

SUNKEN GARDENS, right, on Fourth Street in downtown St. Petersburg abounds with colorful, lush, semitropical foliage. Lovely vistors Cricket Ault and Candy Sugarek take time out to play peek-a-boo with their reflections in a sparkling pound in the Sunken Gardens. (Dunn)

A MEMORABLE DAY IN 1948 was Festival of States Parade. Our photographer was on hand to record the gala event. *Above:* the City of Tampa float on the foreground. *Below:* A well-drilled band cavorts in front of the Alexander Hotel on Central Avenue. (Burgert)

MAAS BROTHERS Department Store, long an institution in Tampa, expanded to other Florida cities after World War II. Here's a picture of the St. Petersburg store, taken on February 27, 1948. (Burgert)

"DARING" TWO-PIECE SUITS came into fashion in 1952 when this fine view of the North Yacht Basin Beach was made. The Million Dollar Pier is in the background. (Burgert)

"MOM" ABERLE and the Jolly Kitchenaires were regular performers at amateur shows on the Million Dollar Pier in 1953. They entertained thousands by playing music on kitchen utensils. (Dunn)

CENTRAL AVENUE AT FOURTH STREET in the 1950s before the First Federal Building and Loan Association modernized its building (at right). The pretty Spanish-looking building is the Rutland Building, formerly Snell Arcade, a boom-time landmark. (Burgert)

HISTORY IN THE MAKING was taking place as the photographer recorded engineers putting into place the last section of the Sunshine Skyway Bridge in the Spring of 1971. The toll span between St. Petersburg and Bradenton was first opened in 1954. It originally was a two-lane span, but the four lane bridge was constructed as traffic picked up. The distinctive bridge is so high it permits ocean-going vessels to go underneath. The bridge is formally named to honor the late William Dean, one of the first State engineers to do extensive work with prestressed concrete. (Dunn)